Praise for *Winds of Spirit*

"A unique and fascinating book to help you reset your inner compass and navigate the uncharted seas of your life. Winds of Spirit invites you to meet the wind gods of ancient times who will help you find grace and wisdom in any situation if you invoke them. A truly magical book for the modern seeker."

— **Colette Baron-Reid**, best-selling author of
Messages from Spirit, The Map, and *Uncharted*

*"*Winds of Spirit *is a fabulous book that will transform you into a lover of the wind. Renee Baribeau is an exquisite wordsmith. Her writing emerges from the depth of her heart and soul as she writes about her life experience and how she healed herself. She shares such awe-inspiring legends and practices of how to work with the wind to navigate life, heal from your past, and invoke blessings. This is truly one of the best books I have read. It is inspiring and unique."*

— **Sandra Ingerman**, author of *Soul Retrieval* and *Walking in Light*

"Beautifully written. Truly inspiring. Practical and applicable. This book will help guide you to the true path of finding your own inner wisdom and verified faith. Read it, apply the wisdom, and together we shall create a positive change on this planet from the inside out."

— **Noah Levine**, author of *Dharma Punx*

*"*Winds of Spirit *is a fascinating guide to working with the wind. This is a must-read for anyone wanting to enhance their knowledge of its ancient wisdom."*

— **Joan Borysenko, Ph.D.**, *New York Times*
best-selling author of *Minding the Body, Mending the Mind*

"Renee shares so much of herself and her hard-won wisdom in this well-written and enlightening book."

— **Mackenzie Phillips**, actress and singer

"Winds of Spirit *is a beautiful and thought-provoking book that presents the winds as transpersonal forces of nature that live around and within us throughout our lives. This absorbing book held my interest to the last page, and reveals Renee Baribeau as a modern, western medicine woman.*"

— **Hank Wesselman, Ph.D.**, anthropologist, shamanist teacher, and author of *The Re-Enchantment*, the award-winning *Awakening to the Spirit World* (with Sandra Ingerman), *The Bowl of Light*, and the critically acclaimed Spiritwalker trilogy

"Praises to Renee Baribeau for blowing a gust of fresh wind into the rich shamanic body of wisdom. This book masterfully reconnects us to the wind gods and goddesses, and steers us to think and develop an intimate relationship with that life-giving and destructive force, one we may take for granted. Read this remarkable book."

— **Itzhak Beery**, author of *The Gift of Shamanism*, *Shamanic Transformations*, and *Shamanic Healing*

"Renee has masterfully enlaced cultural knowledge and practices, bringing us a new global vision of the wind spirits to help us navigate our tumultuous times toward a more beautiful tomorrow."

— **Elizabeth B. Jenkins**, best-selling author of *The Return of the Inka*

"Renee Baribeau has written a must-read primer for anyone considering their own spiritual evolution. I was riveted by the depth of her myths, legends, and sacred stories. Her work is not only a scholarly treatise on the resilience of the human spirit, but a deeply evocative narrative that bore her vulnerability with a sense of power and dignity. Her use of ancient storytelling had me sitting on the edge of my seat. The reader is served by her eloquence, imagination, and authentic truth telling. For some readers, the entire book will lead to an inner awakening and a revelation of all that is holy."

— **Dr. Sharron Stroud**, president of the International Foundation for World Peace and Research and spiritual leader of Innerfaith New Thought Spiritual Center Worldwide

WINDS
OF
SPIRIT

Hay House Titles of Related Interest

YOU CAN HEAL YOUR LIFE, the movie,
starring Louise Hay & Friends
(available as a 1-DVD program, an expanded
2-DVD set, and an online streaming video)
Learn more at www.hayhouse.com/louise-movie

THE SHIFT, the movie,
starring Dr. Wayne W. Dyer
(available as a 1-DVD program, an expanded
2-DVD set, and an online streaming video)
Learn more at www.hayhouse.com/the-shift-movie

***

ONE SPIRIT MEDICINE: Ancient Ways to Ultimate Wellness,
by Alberto Villoldo

*IT'S NOT THE END OF THE WORLD: Developing Resilience
in Times of Change,* by Joan Borysenko, Ph.D.

SHAMANISM: Awaken and Develop the Shamanic Force Within,
by Christa Mackinnon

*KINDLING THE NATIVE SPIRIT: Sacred Practices
for Everyday Life,* by Denise Linn

All of the above are available at your local bookstore,
or may be ordered by visiting:

Hay House USA: www.hayhouse.com®
Hay House Australia: www.hayhouse.com.au
Hay House UK: www.hayhouse.co.uk
Hay House India: www.hayhouse.co.in

WINDS
OF
SPIRIT

Ancient Wisdom Tools for Navigating
Relationships, Health, and the Divine

RENEE BARIBEAU

HAY HOUSE, INC.
Carlsbad, California • New York City
London • Sydney • New Delhi

Published in the United States by: Hay House, Inc.: www.hayhouse.com®
Published in Australia by: Hay House Australia Pty. Ltd.: www.hayhouse.com.au
Published in the United Kingdom by: Hay House UK, Ltd.: www.hayhouse.co.uk
Published in India by: Hay House Publishers India: www.hayhouse.co.in

Cover design: Amy Grigoriou • *Interior design:* Karim J. Garcia

Cataloging-in-Publication Data is on file at the Library of Congress

Tradepaper ISBN: 978-1-4019-5275-4

1st edition, February 2018

Printed in the United States of America

To the winds that have stirred
my imagination from my first breath.

CONTENTS

PART IV: THE INNER WINDS—FORCES OF NATURE

WIND SONG

The wind is the whisper of our mother the earth
The wind is the hand of our father the sky
The wind watches over our struggles and pleasures
The wind is the goddess who first learned to fly

The wind is the bearer of bad and good tidings
The weaver of darkness, bringer of dawn
The wind gives the rain, then builds us a rainbow
The wind is the singer who sang the first song

The wind is a twister of anger and warning
The wind brings the fragrance of freshly mown hay
The wind is a racer, and a wild stallion running
The sweet taste of love on a slow summer's day

The wind knows the songs of the cities and canyons
The thunder of mountains, roar of the sea
The wind is the taker and giver of mornings
The wind is the symbol of all that is free

So welcome the wind and the wisdom she offers
Follow her summons when she calls again
In your heart and your spirit let the breezes surround you
Lift up your voice then and sing with the wind

— JOHN DENVER AND JOE HENRY

INTRODUCTION

Navigating Change

In the beginning, there was wind.
Then they went silent . . . until now.

Wind is the invisible force of nature whose thumbprint leaves an indelible mark on time and space. The art of navigating the earth's windswept landscape has preoccupied humankind throughout history. Animals such as reindeer naturally alter migration routes based on changing weather patterns and conditions, while human beings seek ways to better understand and control their surroundings. Long ago our ancestors lived in harmony with the earth; they navigated experience by relying on their senses, and by cooperating with the soul of nature in order to identify, invoke, pursue, or create a better way of life for their communities. With the mass exodus from the farmlands to the city, many lost their way.

Wind existed first, took care of Earth when it appeared, and then informed humans how to see and navigate.[1] As new cultures emerged from Africa, Egypt, Northern Europe, and the South Seas, the wind gods and goddesses played a prominent role in cosmogony and mythology. Do these myths allude to the beginning of the cosmos, or do they tell the story of a specific era in ancient history? Could we be looking at a grand 2,160-year astrological cycle of the universe when people were awake and living in harmony with nature, and then were lulled back to sleep after eating a poisoned apple? And now, faced with Anthropocene, are we slowly awaking from a deep sleep?

Great ideas are born of the wind, and have always been available to those whose inner eyes and ears are open. While I was conducting scholarly and phenomenological research for this book, these sacred winds made unexpected appearances. In 2016, a mysterious temple that scientists believe was used to worship Ehécatl-Quetzalcoatl, the Aztec wind god, was uncovered during the demolition of a supermarket in Mexico City. The following year, another Aztec artifact, an inscribed Jade pendant, was found in Belize, more than sixty miles from the original Mayan center of influence. Scientists believe that this magical pendant tells a powerful story dedicated to the wind god, Ehécatl-Quetzalcoatl, and the demise of the Aztec civilization.[2] Early on, during my study of these ancient wind practices, I was enchanted by the sound of a whistle while visiting the Mesoamerican valley and temple of Teotihuacan. I believe that these separate events are connected.

In every age and region, we have sought to understand our purpose for living by seeking within. On a personal level, this inward journey has led me to the Amazon jungle in Peru, to perform hiking initiations with shamans in the Andes, and to pursue Native American vision quests in the wilderness of North America. Taking journeys of self-discovery such as these are not always feasible for everyone, but we can all do something to get our bearings every day.

Seeking to understand the mysteries of life and to give meaning to our experiences is human nature. In *Winds of Spirit*, I invite you to venture into and explore your inner world, a veritable holographic representation of the outer world that surrounds you, by invoking wind deities—gods and goddesses from around the world—and the cardinal winds from the four quadrants of the sky. These four quadrants are the mind, emotions, body, and spirit, and they all relate to the inner landscape of your life. By offering a means to identify coordinates on the map of your life and to assess prevailing conditions, this system will help you to navigate your personal path and provide insight into how to manage the wind patterns and shifting conditions that affect you.

Although the wind work system is new, it relies on an ancient one that has been used for centuries by shamans for ritual, and by sailors for navigation of the seas. Like the shamans and sailors, we can rely on wind, a natural force, for guidance. To orient our life, instead of using the magnetized needle of the compass, or a lodestone to point to a fixed pole, we can utilize the intelligence and astute sensitivity of our own bodies. *Winds of Spirit* will teach you how to connect with your true inner self, your spiritual magnetic north. By viewing the world from the perspective of this "sweet spot," you will safely navigate your way through life and never get lost.

The ideas in this book are rooted in ancient sailing practices, so nautical and meteorological terms are used to describe many concepts. No matter what wind may be blowing, traversing any situation is possible if you have the proper bearings. Although this is easy to say, becoming a competent navigator of daily life takes practice and persistence. In life, as in sailing, adverse conditions are common, but informed responses always lead to safety. Sometimes your boat will get tossed about in the powerful squalls, filling up with water, but with the use of proper navigational tools, you will find your way to clear blue skies, calm waters, and safe harbors.

Since 2005, I have worked as a shamanic healer in Palm Desert, California. My journey on the path to energy work began one cool night in 1994 during a fire-walking ceremony. I experienced trust exercises, chanting, and other mind-bending tricks designed to raise the personal vibrations and power of the group energy. After several hours, we walked over red-hot coals without burning our feet. That night, a bonfire was lit in my soul. I no longer believed my world was flat, or that I was destined to live the life of alcoholism and depression that had plagued me since adolescence. I now knew unequivocally that there was much more to life than I had imagined.

Hungry for esoteric knowledge, I sought out teachings from every tradition that crossed my path. My search led me west to California, where I began my shamanic training. For years, I apprenticed with a local Lakota Sioux elder, praying in Inipi ceremonies.

The adventure continued, and I trekked with shamans in Chile, Mexico, and Peru. Despite my reluctance to become a healer, I was encouraged by my mentors to take a two-year course in shamanic healing. After completing this program, clients began to appear in my life. Over the years, I became known as the practical shaman because of my emphasis on finding effective tools that could be used to improve the quality of everyday life for business professionals.

I quickly realized the majority of my clients would not be willing to brave rigorous shamanic healing initiations. People often told me they wanted to explore the *whys* of their lives, but they needed a simple way to do so. Despite mastering the how-tos of career, family, and finances, most people said there was an unidentified "something more" or "something else" they were supposed to be doing, but they lacked direction to find it. They wanted a new way to respond to events and desires, but felt stressed, disconnected, and distracted. With their concerns in mind, I had a vision in which I was shown a new guidance system that would teach others how to access the wisdom that resides within all of us. Form follows thought, and the very act of setting this goal caused an east wind to rustle the leaves of awareness in my consciousness. I became inspired to create a healing system that would enable ordinary people—even spiritual novices—to do valuable energy work with little training.

The element missing in most people's lives is a simple direct way to access presence—the here and now. Every moment is a time-space intersection. When we locate ourselves in the present, we gain clarity that allows us to move forward with purpose. Living with awareness in the present can be likened to a sheet pinned to a clothesline flapping in the breeze. I wondered, *Can we pin ourselves to the present without having to resort to austere spiritual training?*

One day, while hiking along the cliffs overlooking the Pacific Ocean at Ebey's Landing National Historical Reserve in Washington State, I listened to the wind howling through the Douglas firs. As it buffeted me, I realized that being able to bend with the wind is not enough. We should also be able to move gracefully through our lives like sailboats. Yet, as we do so, different energies impact us. Some of these forces are external and some come from within. Every moment is an opportunity for us to reset our inner compass, not only in space and time, but also physically, mentally, emotionally, and spiritually. Navigation is a creative act. By responding appropriately to the various winds that blow through our lives, we can become adept sailors, capable of navigating to any destination of our choosing.

How do we navigate in the wind? Do we need to have a fixed object to guide us, like the North Star, which ancient sailors used? What is our fixed object? Soon after pondering these questions, while participating in a shamanic ceremony in Mexico, the idea of using the body as a compass for navigating through life was revealed to me. The human body is always fixed in the present. Thus, it is the needle in the compass that points northward toward an awakening. In the same way that ancient mariners utilized handheld compasses to chart their course, we can also use our bodies as powerful, precise instruments of navigation.

From that day forward, the parallels between energy and wind made themselves known to me. I had a notion of where my journey of discovery would take me, and faith that I was headed for a fragrant new world, but like a fifteenth-century sailor, I had no idea where this landmass was located. For this reason, I asked, *Is there a way to be totally present during moments of anxiety, turbulence, and chaos? If so, what would that look like?* As I answered these and other questions, I started to recognize patterns in the complex dynamics of the art of living.

My research into the history of compasses led me to the world of winds. I explored a variety of sources ranging from books, movies, and pop culture, to the legends and mythology of world cultures—particularly ancient and indigenous societies. I learned that the breath of mythological wind beings has impacted every culture on Earth. As the wind carried my hot air balloon of inspiration higher and higher, I realized there was much more to the energies of emotion and thought than I had first imagined. After hundreds of hours of research that barely scratched the surface of these stories, I realized wind energy is more than a metaphor—it is a literal force of nature. Working with clients showed me the path, as they began experiencing the wind deities as dynamic living archetypes of spirit. During sessions with my clients, the winds came whenever they were called. Beyond noticing the rustling of leaves, clients would experience these deities directly, as feelings inside their bodies, as visual images in their mind's eye, and with mysterious synchronicity. They continued to share similar stories that complemented my vision when I played the ancient wind instrument. Patterns of resistance were described as literally falling away during their encounter with the emanating wind energy.

Wind has life-giving properties. When we breathe, our lungs take in oxygen-rich air created by plants that thrive on the carbon dioxide exhaled by humans and other creatures. The wind carries the air everywhere on Earth. Each of us is, therefore, part of an energetic cycle that extends beyond plants and animals, into the oceans and upper layers of the atmosphere. Ancient cultures may not have completely understood the science of exchange between life-forms, but they were keenly aware of the principles of nature, and incorporated them into their lives much better than we do today.

The mythology of wind from different cultures indicate one unifying principle. Our ancient ancestors knew that whenever someone tries to control the wind, stagnation and death soon follow. Wind is a mighty force that can be destructive, but can also be a powerful ally. Thus, it is essential that we learn to live in harmony with it. Too much wind energy and we're overwhelmed; too little and we become depleted.

Winds of Spirit can teach you how to recognize and utilize the subtle energies in your life to heal yourself. Healing—or becoming more aligned with the fullness of us, and our purpose for being—is a lifelong journey. Our greatest gifts are sometimes accompanied by thunderous squalls that push us away from our intended plans and destinations. Change can often be initiated by a gentle breeze nudging us in a new direction.

SETTING SAIL

To become a competent navigator of daily life, one must practice, be persistent, and have a reliable map. Maps are used for planning a new route, creating spatial awareness, and for finding one's way when lost. My hope is that *Winds of Spirit* will become your cherished map and a constant companion for navigating change as you journey through life.

Adventures often begin with preplanning and preparation. Although the concepts and ideas in this book are ancient, they offer a fresh and unique perspective on how to live in today's world. I invite you to start at the beginning of the book and allow the winds of your imagination to stir as they move you through all the chapters. Once you grasp the basics of wind science, my hope is that the wind gods and goddesses described in Part IV will become your trusted allies.

We begin with Part I, which lays the groundwork for the wind work system, offering you basic wind meteorology as it applies to your life. The journey begins with you, an earth traveler, waking up, then remembering the ancient wisdom and weather forecasting tools. During each of the three stages of awakening, these winds of spirit can provide a meaningful context in which to order your life. You will learn about three types of winds: cardinal compass winds, inner winds, and global winds. Practical application is key to the success of any useful system, and in *Winds of Spirit* you will learn how to harness these powerful forces of nature and use them to your advantage as you navigate change in your daily life.

In Part II, you'll gain insight into recurring themes found in the human experiences. These cardinal winds have held up the sky and the four pillars of spatial experience since time immemorial. The compass card winds represent the cardinal directions and the cycles of life: birth, expansion, death, and decay. As you begin to understand the foundational principles that organize human experience, you will become adept at navigating change. East represents the mind, memories, and new beginnings; south is the land of emotions, needs, and desires; west relates to physical bodies, harvests, and endings; and north pertains to spirituality and community. The cardinal directional winds provide an overview of the landscape, and how they can help shape your body into a finely tuned compass.

This brings us to Part III. Part III offers practical tools, and exercises derived from a variety of ancient cultures that will keep you on course when the winds of change begin to stir. You can consistently reach your goals by honing your navigational skills.

Finally, Part IV is designed to provide ongoing guidance. These 29 cross-cultural inner winds are conscious forces of divine energy that directly influence your thoughts, feelings, and actions. While I do not claim to have complete knowledge of the cultures from which each wind originates, I have tried my best to conduct a scholarly and phenomenological research of each wind god and goddess. Through the process of uncovering these ancient deities, I realized that all humans are affected by the same wind. Beyond all of the cultural context, wind consciousness influences every event under heaven. All ideas are born of the wind, and have been in the air since long before humans inhabited the planet. The power and wisdom of wind binds and interconnects us.

Winds of Spirit is ancient and sacred knowledge. You can randomly open any page in Part IV whenever you need guidance. Trust the process. The wind knows what you need in every moment.

Once you begin to read these pages and are open to their life-changing messages, your relationship with wind will be forever changed. You will witness the power of these powerful, churning forces of nature as they impact your physical, emotional, mental, and spiritual bodies. Whenever the wind blows into your life, it is time to pause and ask, "What is the message for me in this time and space called *now*?"

Part I

THE
WINDS OF
CHANGE

CHAPTER I

THE GOAL:
THE AWAKENED SELF

"It just takes one moment of new perception to change a life."[1]
— MARION WOODMAN

Awakening is a natural process, and wind is the sacred mediator. The transition from sleep to wakefulness happens every morning. Before you wake up, your breath deepens. Then you become conscious and open your eyes.

Awakening in a spiritual sense is a similar consciousness-raising activity. Invisible forces unite and animate all matter. As we observe our breathing—the core experience we may have of our own life force—we enhance our ability to perceive the movement of the energy inside and around us. Over time, our deepening awareness makes us more capable of navigating the changing conditions in our lives peacefully and successfully. We begin to know ourselves as parts of the whole of nature.

Many people spend years seeking a path toward wholeness. Becoming present with the winds blowing through our lives is a path that can help us heal body and mind, restore balance when it is lost, and guide our creativity.

Here is a way to experience the winds right now. Simply inhale, catching (but not forcing) air into your lungs, letting your abdomen inflate. Hold this life force inside you for a few moments. Then raise a hand and place it near your open mouth. As you gradually exhale, feel the steady wind created by your breath. This wind breath connects you to the moving air in the atmosphere that circumnavigates the globe every few days. During the course of its existence, the energy and molecules of your wind breath will subtly touch every other living being on the planet—plants, animals, people, and even rocks.

Full-scale awakening can take many years. In general, waking up occurs in three stages: first there is self-awareness awakening, which is followed by spiritual awakening, and then radical awakening.

SELF-AWARENESS AWAKENING: LIFE FLOWS LIKE THE WIND

In childhood, I developed obsessive tendencies while waiting hours for my estranged father to arrive for a visit. To soothe myself, I would repeat nonsensical phrases and count the cars that drove by. At age 30, these types of compulsive coping skills were sabotaging my career as a chef. Every morning I would pace back and forth in front of the small restaurant I owned, waiting for my most loyal employee to arrive, and then proceed to remind him of his shortcomings. My controlling behavior gradually pushed him and all my other staff toward the exit door. For five years, my restaurant's reputation had flourished even as I slowly died inside. Running it demanded a level of business acumen I did not yet possess. There were bills to pay, meals to prepare, staff to manage, and customers to wow. What the patrons could not see beneath the perfectly presented plates of food I served them was brewing anger, selfishness, and a growing despondency.

My father then died abruptly, ending our difficult relationship. The winds of spirit motivated me to take action. I visited several doctors, wellness practitioners, and psychics, and attended 12-step meetings to deal with my issues with substance abuse. During the first raw days of sobriety, it was as if a tornado ravaged my inner landscape. The winds were so intense that eventually I decided to spend two weeks recuperating in a mental hospital.

During one of our regular walks, the hospital psychiatrist suggested that finding answers to my problems required reconciliation with my past. It was good advice, but I was not ready for it. His words left me feeling stranded. I could not move forward because I was unable to forgive others or myself for events of long ago.

Eight years later, while driving along a country road, the wind inside me shifted. I was driving with a friend in her gray 1969 Datsun convertible under a wind-tempered sun, along the back roads of Route 20. It was the perfect central New York day for a top-down excursion. Black-spotted dairy cows ambled across the fields. I lifted my head toward the heavens and felt the warmth on my skin. Suddenly, a glimmering wind exploded in the center of my being and illuminated my consciousness. In that moment, I saw billowing clouds moving apart and revealing the cerulean blue of a clear sky. For the first time in my life, I *knew* that I did not want to engage in self-destructive addictive behaviors anymore. It was as if a fog that had been blinding my vision of who I "could be" was instantly lifted. This moment of clarity was so intense that it served as the catalyst for a 25-year adventure to heighten my consciousness further.

For most of us, the urge to "wake up" is evoked by an experience that profoundly disturbs us or interferes with the progress of our lives. Longing for deeper connection creates an opportunity for us to change and do things differently or move in a new direction. Because we must be willing to change, experiencing the self as seeker, is typically the first stage of awakening. It can provide the necessary wind power to invoke forward motion.

Self-awareness that does not lead us to take action will ultimately be fruitless. Engaging in spiritual practices is essential if we are going to become true masters of the winds in our lives. Even so, mastering our powerful inner winds is an incremental process. Just as one must train to scale one of the Seven Summits by hiking smaller mountains first, we must practice wind work during breezes and while in the doldrums so as to learn to keep our sailboats upright when navigating squalls and hurricanes. Self-awareness must become a habit. With each passing windstorm, you will become more capable of flowing with the prevailing energy inside and around you. The quest to find peace is akin to the wind, growing in intensity and speed, as it gathers force with practice.

SPIRITUAL AWAKENING:
DEVELOPING SPIRITUAL RESILIENCE

Spiritual awakening happens when we become willing to take the next step—or sometimes it's enough to be *willing to be willing*, if this is the most we can offer to the awakening process. This is progress.

During the first rocky steps in my recovery from alcoholism, the winds battered me and disrupted my serenity. Despite being told that I could be peaceful no matter what was going on in my life, I did not know how to achieve inner peace. I struggled with my obsession for perfection. Knowing that I was willing—and wanted—to experience the divine and become a more accepting, graceful, and flowing wind made all the difference.

In many myths, wind gods and goddesses live in high mountain caves. Attempting to control nature, the protagonist undertakes a rigorous climb to block wind holes with rocks, fabric, or, in the Hopi tale, cornmeal. Within days of sealing a cave's entrance, wind energy ceases and death soon follows. Survival requires inner personal transformation, cooperation, and acceptance of ever-shifting winds. The villager always returns to the cave and purposely unleashes the powerful wind allies. Like the village hero, working with your winds of change will require you to visit your inner cave to develop and strengthen your resolve. During this stage of awakening, you will develop spiritual resilience by learning to cooperate with nature.

We will now explore your inner cave by practicing inner skills such as surrender, acceptance, devotion, forgiveness, mindfulness, and refining your mind-set to incorporate and allow for the possibility of grace.

Surrender: According John 3:8 (The New King James Version), the wind blows wherever it pleases. Since the winds of spirit move at will, the daily practice of surrender will help you to maintain harmony and balance both in nature and in your life. Surrender involves recognition, followed by conscious action. The degree of your attachment to something defines the time and depth of letting go if you lose it. Surrender involves sacrificing your goals to the divine winds of spirit. For example, when my longtime feline friend Dash passed away, I grieved for six months. The first step in my healing was to see how I had projected all my ideas of love onto a calico cat. When I was finally ready to let go of my pain, I climbed a mountain, where I performed a ritual and cast my friend's ashes to the wind. The winds can help you learn the art of surrender.

Acceptance: An old Chinese proverb teaches, "When the wind of change blows, some people build walls, others build windmills." Time does not stand idly by waiting for you to find acceptance. When my father succumbed to death, destructive winds howled though my life. After many nightlong cocaine and alcohol binges, the pain of our strained relationship remained unresolved. The only option I had to save myself and my restaurant from crumbling was acceptance of my loss—and my imperfections. Regardless of what is happening in your life or what you are doing that you do not like, do your best to be kind to yourself, and try not to get discouraged. Whether you are self-conscious about your weight, addicted, suffering, in a relationship, not in a relationship, lazy, an overachiever, or underemployed, acceptance of your current situation is essential before you can change it.

Acceptance is a process. Imagine yourself speeding along a freeway. To exit, you have to slow down to access the off-ramp safely. As you awaken, you will realize it's time to change certain character traits, but first you must slow down and accept your current coordinates. Some personality traits may shift easily upon awakening, while others may linger. Self-acceptance may require you to seek counseling or other modes of treatment. Just remember you are worth the effort. Trust that acceptance will arrive in its own perfect time.

Devotion: As per Swami Vivekananda, *bhakti* (devotion) "is intense love, which has to be directed toward God."[2] When I was beginning my spiritual journey, an astrologer suggested that my *dharma* (path) in this lifetime was to be committed to spirit, above all else. The idea of being committed to spirit sounded like a cool path. Little did I know at the time that this would require dancing with the wind on top of tall mountains whenever spirit called! It has involved a life with as much silence as interaction with others. Sacrifices have included spirit-directed living, continuous study, prayer, meditation, and hard work. At no point along the journey were favors promised in exchange for my unconditional love.

The path of spiritual awakening requires you to make a commitment to practice a set of actions, with the intention of increasing your capacity for internal happiness. Storms may come and shake your house, but if your foundation is strong and your house is built on faith, it will not fall.

Devotional acts might be small, simple, and repetitive, like looking for meaningful coincidences in seemingly random occurrences in nature, or beginning each day on your knees in prayer; attending a weekly support group, or touching mala beads while repeating a mantra 108 times. A chemotherapy patient I counseled began praying each night before she went to sleep, and her fear of death gradually subsided. Try picking one activity in which you are willing to engage joyfully for four minutes per day, for a week. After seven days, add another stretch of time, or another devotional act to your regimen. Go slowly. By dedicating yourself to a devotional practice that suits your lifestyle, you will become more resilient in the face of the prevailing winds. You may find yourself joyfully dancing with the winds.

Forgiveness: A Persian parable by Malba Tahan teaches, "When someone hurts us, we should write it down in sand, where the winds of forgiveness can erase it away."*

---

* Adapted from a story *Learning to Write in the Sand,* attributed to Malba Tahan. Malba Tahan was a pseudonym of Júlio César de Mello e Souza, 1895–1974, a widely traveled Brazilian mathematics professor.

Forgiveness neutralizes painful events. Anger and resentment are disturbing states of mind that become increasingly uncomfortable winds as you awaken. *Resentment* comes from Latin, meaning *to refeel*. How can you be present and awake when you are recycling old stories? Forgiveness is an action that requires you to recognize self-defeating wind patterns and take inventory of your own imperfections, as well as to bear witness to the perpetrators' deed(s). Until you can see the role you play in each life experience, and the gift received by virtue of others' behavior, you will remain in limbo. Every outward action from another is a mirror to help you grow spiritually.

That said, the deeper the wound, the longer the healing process may take. Forgiveness allows you to feel compassion for another's misgivings, but it does not mean you will forget (although you *can*); nor does it encourage the continuation of unhealthy relationships. Still, even the worst life experiences may provide valuable insights. For example, my challenging childhood prepared me to explore the depths of my resolve, and eventually I became a compassionate healer. Your beloved pet may pass away and provide you with a spiritual lesson; the death of a loved one can alter your life path toward divine service; being sexually abused as a child can provide the impetus to help others heal; and loving an addict may expand your capacity for compassion.

If you seek serenity, it is important to make peace with everything and everybody. If you find this difficult, consider a 12th-century Germanic belief that says you can get rid of a cold by giving it to someone else.[3] If this holds true, giving pardon to someone else will also relieve you from burden. Similarly, there is a saying in Alcoholics Anonymous: "Fake it 'til you make it." This expression has merit.

You are whole and complete within yourself. Once you realize that life flows like the wind, you will begin the long journey of forgiveness, a move that will magically transform you from crazy self-centered thinking to unconditional love of the situations and people in your life. Forgiveness is an ongoing process that will continue as you expand your spiritual faculties. Over time, you will forgive yourself, family, friends, perpetrators, and God, thus opening the pathways toward a radical awakening. You will learn that every wind that has ever blown through your life and altered your landscape has been for your benefit and personal spiritual growth.

Mindfulness: Thich Nhat Hanh tells us, "Feelings come and go like clouds in a windy sky. Conscious breathing is my anchor."[4] Mindfulness is a state of consciousness that focuses on the prevailing wind. Wind flows presently. You cannot fly a kite with yesterday's breath, and tomorrow's gales are no help. Waking up requires consciously shifting your attention back toward the present zephyr. Even after hiking an ice-capped mountain, spending time in silent retreats, and undertaking many spiritual adventures, extended periods of peace eluded me. At last, one day, I experienced the company of a strawberry I had picked from my own garden. In that moment, I realized I had chased serenity for decades, in workshops and across the continents. Then I found it, waiting in my own yard. In that moment, there was only myself and a juicy morsel.

Moving from a tornado of obsessive thinking to a place of stillness requires patience, persistence, and practice. For me, the first glimmer of serenity arrived on a cold night in northern Vermont after spending time with chanting monks. I bathed in the winds of silence under a star-filled sky. I cherished those moments when I could taste fleeting stillness, the subtle flavor of which inadvertently got watered down by the hustle and bustle of life. Over time, each mindful step I took reinforced the last, and the moments grew exponentially into days, then weeks, and even months.

Although mindfulness meditation may be an important element of your daily practice, more effort is required. Mindfulness is about living life on life's terms, no matter what intensity of wind is upon you, be it doldrums, trade winds, or storm winds, in every moment and in every experience. The goal is to remain steadfast even when strong winds threaten to topple your dreams. The mindfulness muscle strengthens over time. To wake up, you must apply your practice of mindfulness to every area of your life: cooking, cleaning, working, relationships, driving a car, shopping, and paying bills.

Preparation for living mindfully can be rehearsed in 12-step meetings and meditation groups; by repeating mantras, offering prayers of gratitude, and walking in nature; through participating in study groups, making medicine wheels, and attending church or purification ceremonies; and through wind practices. The sweet fruit may be hanging just beyond your grasp.

Many people are content to remain at the stage of spiritual awakening for decades. They have found considerable relief from their pain, and employing the above actions has increased their resilience. But traveling farther along the path of awakening, and becoming truly obedient to the guidance of spirit, requires the winds of grace. For me, when I climbed halfway up Machu Picchu, the winds demanded that I continue the trek even though I was tempted to give up. "Renee, enlightenment is not found halfway up the mountain," they bellowed in my ears. Despite the agony of my aching limbs, and the doubts that I could reach the top, I inched my way to the summit, where I beheld the beautiful panoramic view of the mighty Amazon River below.

From this single point of consciousness emerged a possibility for entirely new outcomes in my life. I completed a strenuous five-day trek through the mountain. My illusion of being disconnected from the talking rocks, the winds, and other people was shattered. Everything felt connected by the wind's breath. At last I perceived my oneness with nature and felt whole. This was my first experience toward a radical awakening.

RADICAL AWAKENING:
INTEGRATING THREE LEVELS OF AWARENESS

Radical awakening is a profound shift of consciousness that occurs when your subconscious mind, conscious mind, and superconscious mind are in alignment and grace intercedes.

Although rare, some people move directly to radical awakening. When they do, their lives are altered forever. This phenomenon has been reported by people who have had near-death experiences, or *shaktipat* (when the winds of grace enter your consciousness and fill you, either through a divine transmission from a guru or god), or through deep meditational states. For me, the transformation came after many years of deep personal work with plant medicine. I was ready for the shift in consciousness that comes with being fully awake. After a challenging healing session in which a crystallized energy block the size of a cowlick was pulled from my solar plexus, I felt empty. Soon afterward I was filled with translucent colored winds: blue, green, gold, and purple. From that day forward, I was consistently peaceful, present, and happy.

You can establish conditions for radical awakening to occur. As part of my recovery, I conducted a thorough inventory of my past behaviors. Then I traveled 3,000 miles to make amends to different people for my past self-serving behaviors. One apology was owed to a young man, a former employee, now dead, whom I had verbally abused every day for two years. The day after I visited his grave, I paid my respects to a former landlord who lived in another town 100 miles away. After our meeting, I decided to walk through the town. Upon randomly entering a store, I encountered the mother of the young man whose grave I had visited in the cemetery. This was a jaw-dropping example of synchronicity. After I explained to her that I had flown from California to upstate New York to clean up the wreckage of my past, including making amends to her son, she took my hand and said, "He forgives you and that is why I am here." In that moment, I felt washed clean by the winds of grace. While she had done the legwork for forgiveness to occur, it was an unmerited gift from God that allowed me to witness the transformation. This is grace.

Through the process of taking inventory—of reliving chronic misery and pain—I experienced a radical awakening. No longer could I harm another, or myself, for I saw us as the same. From that day forward, self-seeking behaviors began to slip naturally away, replaced by a willingness to be of service to others. For the first time, I became a willing servant of the winds.

The results of your awakening are beautiful. People around you also awaken. Family members you once mistrusted become allies. You have no difficulty accepting your friends and partners as they are. You are present to all life. You understand that everything is connected and equal. When the wind blows particularly hard, you lower the sails, brace yourself, and wait patiently, knowing that every storm will eventually move on and reveal a clear blue sky.

In their ancient mythology, our ancestors from Africa, Egypt, Northern Europe, and the Americas described three realms of awareness—a tri-part world of sky, earth, and caves that led to the lower world. The heavens were home to the sky gods. The earth was the home of people, plants, and animals. The inner crust of the earth was the place for dreamers and the dead. According to the Q'ero of Peru, these are the *ukhupacha*, or inner (lower) world, the *kaypacha*, or everyday reality (middle world), and the *hanan pacha*, or upper world of infinite wisdom. Cosmologies of different communities used different terminology to describe these three levels of existence. The goal of awakening through wind work is to have a functional relationship with the energy from all three domains.

To become a fully conscious human being and experience radical awakening, you must spend time exploring your subconscious, conscious, and superconscious minds and learn how to integrate their energy into all areas of your life.

INTEGRATING SUBCONSCIOUS AWARENESS USING WIND WORK

Once you begin cooperating with your cardinal and inner winds, self-defeating emotional patterns that litter your subconscious will begin to stir, causing resistance that will get your attention. These intuitive signals and any physical ailments provide early weather alerts that something needs to change. Threadbare ideas and emotions will not endure the storm, and the grit in your shoes will cause you to pause and reflect. Wind moves hidden agendas into the light of day. Awareness will fill your sail, and you will begin to change self-defeating behaviors as you shift your thoughts and feelings toward beneficial actions.

Many wind gods, including the Aztec wind god Ehécatl, had to visit the domain of the subconscious (underworld) many times to shed light on their own character flaws. Wind can shred your experience. A metaphoric dismemberment may be required to stitch the pieces back together to create a stronger whole.

Wind gets between the cracks in the rocks and penetrates underground caves. The Basque wind mother Mari reportedly used these underground passageways for safe travel throughout the Pyrenees Mountains. Legend speaks of Mari's ability to shape-shift into animals and other beneficial spirits. Call up the mother to shapeshift your behavior, remove lesser character traits, call back soul parts, or explore your creativity. Her winds of spirit can help you subdue and then shift denser energies of rage and addiction so that depression can be lifted.

Shamans understood that emotionally charged energies stored in the *ukhupacha* could be released and shifted through energy work. Character flaws are like the magnetic pull of the earth; they grow stronger or weaker depending upon your coordinates (spiritual conditioning). Once you cooperate with your inner winds, two things occur: you discover your home center, and you eventually turn outward to be of greater service to others in the world around you.

Invite in the winds of spirit to help you journey to your inner caves. This is a dark, rich space where you can create lasting change.

INTEGRATING CONSCIOUS AWARENESS USING WIND WORK

With the proper tools in hand, and the right attitude, it is possible to emerge from sleep to achieve any goal. We are all familiar with the adage, "Work hard and you will succeed." Free will, in the form of disciplined action and backed by wind, is required to pursue your destiny. Moderation of experience is key. Overwork can be a whirling maelstrom that leads to illness, depression, ongoing frustration, and low self-esteem. Conversely, a positive balanced approach will lead to success.

The work of integrating conscious awareness using wind work begins by learning to stay present in your body. Without conscious awareness, you can easily slip in and out of your body without knowing it. One time, while doing a spiritual home cleanse for a client who was not at home, I became aware that her energy was following me from room to room. The woman had a rigorous workload, and I realized that although she was not physically present, half her energy remained at home. This happens all the time. Accidents, trauma, and overstimulation can cause fragments of the self to "check out."

Wind work can help you stay fully grounded in your body. Exercises like the wind bath (discussed later in this book) can help you stay focused. Activities such as prayer and meditation, or calling to the wind gods/goddess, can help you transcend old self-limiting patterns of behavior. Even when you fall prey to illness and depression, you can become the objective observer and find wisdom blowing in the wind.

INTEGRATING SUPERCONSCIOUS AWARENESS USING WIND WORK

When the universe was created, wind gods/goddesses played an active role. The Hopi wind god Yaponcha was the life-giving breath. The wind goddess Amaunet was the feminine counterpart of Amun, the Egyptian creator god. Working with ancient creator winds will enliven your vision, help you manifest unseen energy into form, and breathe new life into your service work.

Sourcing from your superconscious awareness involves a shift in perception. Self-mastery requires thinking with your whole mind. Superconscious awareness involves knowing what is taking place at every level of your existence. In the Hopi lifeway, people emerged and traveled separately, before rediscovering the cooperative nature of community.[5] Similarly, superconscious awareness is a shift from the personal to the collective winds.

Imagine for a moment that you will be attending a family reunion, when you are informed that an estranged relative whom you have not forgiven will be attending. You become angry. Sourcing from the unconscious leads to a self-righteous tantrum (wind storm) over not getting your way, and you stay home. By viewing the situation from the superconscious perspective, you realize that this event may be the last chance for your entire family to gather. Responding from a place of service will allow you to *soulfully* give your full mental, emotional, physical, and spiritual cooperation to the experience.

Once you become radically awake, it becomes increasingly easy to *respond* instead of *react*. You can put away the past, find your humanity, and rediscover your purpose every single day. This process of completion clears the path for living in harmony with others.

A positive attitude is a key indicator of someone who is radically awake. They give freely instead of looking for handouts. People who are radically awake are compassionate and generous; they do not judge a homeless man sleeping in the street; they may even offer this person food or money. Authentic giving comes from the heart. They understand what it is like to be down and out. While everyone experiences difficult times, these people rarely have a bad day.

Two people might face similar obstacles in life, yet the first may become a pillar of strength, while the other is unable to cope and crumbles under pressure. While death is the inevitable outcome of life, an "awakened" terminally ill individual will rise to the occasion by giving service to the experience. Friends and family may gain a richer life experience as they witness the passing of a loved one who remains curious, calm, and confident throughout treatment.

RIDING THE WIND: GRACE

Awakening is like wind; there are periods during the doldrums when the water is still; storm gusts may require patience while you wait, and trade winds may provide impetus to move forward. In my thirties, my lightning storm manifested as the early death of my father, shortly after I opened my first restaurant. Drugs and alcohol were the potions I used to soothe my feelings and keep success at bay. Like a *paqo* teacher from Peru who was literally struck by lightning when spirit wanted his attention, it took many more claps of thunder to get my attention before I said yes to my life's work as a healer.

The goal of the shaman's spiritual vision is life-centered; the shaman is focused on living in harmony with the blessings found in nature and community. In Peru, the rural, agrarian Andean people are committed to the principle of *Ayni*, or sacred reciprocity. In traditional agrarian societies, people rely on nature and neighbors to plant, grow, and harvest their crops. As conditions shift, they adapt their methods accordingly. The happy people of this culture are mindful of *when* and *how* to change.

As an American shamanic healer, I have witnessed a growing sense of isolation, disharmony, and "stuckness" in our society. Many people find it exceedingly difficult to adapt to rapidly shifting conditions. Despite our ability to communicate globally in seconds via electronic media, we have lost our ability to connect with nature and one another, as well as with our inner selves. Often, we don't realize we are in pain because we are constantly distracted and suppress or ignore our innermost feelings. When we are fully awakened, we can recognize and interpret the signs around and within us, alerting us to why, how, when, and where in our lives we need to adapt and reestablish balance. When we're awakened, it's clear what form of reciprocity needs to be expressed from moment to moment.

During my first visit to Peru, I met Don Manuel Quispe (1905–2004), a teacher of the Q'ero Nation. The Quechua translator told our group that Alto mesayoc, Don Manuel, envisioned Westerners from North America would become the new modern-day shamans. Although I was a novice on the path of awakening, I could feel genuine love. This outpouring of love provided a wind of hope and inspired my returns to Peru many times over the following years. Their ancient indigenous wisdom provided a simple but arduous path up the mountain.

Time to explore ancient wisdom practices and how to apply these tools to your life. Harmonizing with nature can help you cope with loss, heal heartbreak, become present, shift your course, and flow through experience like wind through a willow.

Start your lookout for others who share your goal. It's easy to recognize people who are awake; they ride the winds with passion, their needs are met, they obtain measurable results, and they experience a sense of joy and fulfillment by serving others each and every day.

CHAPTER 2

THE STORY OF WIND: APPLYING ANCIENT KNOWLEDGE TO MODERN-DAY NAVIGATION

Enduring proof that wind and spirit are synonymous is expressed in poetry, ancient ballads, storytelling, and shared rituals. Throughout the ages, oral tradition has served as both an art form and a useful tool for preserving history, mythology, lineage, and law, which otherwise might have been forgotten or lost. Ballads have preserved stories in song because music is rhythmical, and words locked in stanzas are less likely to be changed.

Storytellers have been instrumental in keeping the winds of spirit alive for millennia. One North American legend tells the story of Gluscabi and the wind eagle. A young boy cannot fish because the howling wind is distracting him, and he asks his grandmother where to find the source of these uncomfortable winds. After a long hike, he reaches the top of the mountain, where he meets the culprit, the wind eagle. He tricks the bird, ties him up, and stuffs the feathered creature into a crack in the rocks. Without wind, the air gets hot, the water stagnates, and everything becomes covered with sludge. Upon realizing that life cannot exist without wind, the boy sets out to free the wind eagle.

He realizes that wind is essential; it clears the air we breathe and moves the rain clouds.

Narrative poems are one of the most ancient methods of sharing wind wisdom. In India, Vedic chants, including the *Tara Mantra of Om*, contain metered verses that, when sung, reveal sacred secrets. In Hawaii, sacred stories called *moʻolelo* cultivate values of generosity, loyalty, parental respect, and justice.[1] *The Wind Gourd of Laʻamaomao* (a translation of *Hawaii o Pakaa a me Ku-a-Pakaa, na Kahu Iwikuamoo o Keawenuiaumi, ke Alii o Hawaii, a o na Moopuna hoi a Laamaomao*) is the Hawaiian story of Pakaa and Ku-a-Pakaa, the personal attendants of Keawenuiaumi, the chief of Hawaii, and the descendants of the wind goddess Laʻamaomao, who carries a powerful instrument that enables him to control the wind. The gourd contains the bones of his grandmother and all the winds of Hawaii. Like you, Pakaa's journey requires him to awaken to the proper use of power.

Ritual practices that originate in nature provide a wind of continuity in animism, polytheism, and monotheism. The wind whisperers of Poland have preserved their ritual secrets. For centuries, shamans have been hiding in plain sight, as good neighbors, alongside the rigid dogma of Christianity. Despite religious ridicule and political opposition, these practices have remained intact. The existence of these peasant shamans is a testament to the enduring nature of earth-based traditions.

Ancient poetry, music, and magical practices involving the winds of spirit have endured for more than 10,000 years. Valuable tools and knowledge have been preserved and are available to you at this most crucial time in human history.

HOW THESE WIND GODS/GODDESSES CAN IMPROVE YOUR CURRENT CONDITIONS

Before the establishment of organized religion, people worshipped nature gods and goddesses. It was common practice to offer sacrifices to these celestial entities in return for favors. The only sacrifice the winds in this book seek is for you to open your heart, mind, and soul, while embracing their messages of hope. Their sole purpose is to help you safely navigate the trials and tribulations you encounter as you journey through life.

Here are a few examples of how these ancient ones can help you navigate life: connecting with nature; dealing with loss and grief; healing heartbreak; staying present; changing direction; going with the flow; and enriching your personal relationship to spirit.

Connecting with Nature: In today's modern world, disassociation from nature manifests as depression, anger, addiction, isolation, separation, greed, and war. Opening up to the power and wisdom winds can reconnect us to spirit. Nature gods/goddesses have survived since before Moses and monotheism were introduced in the 13th and 14th centuries BCE, after which time all preceding gods were demoted. While some preserved rank, becoming saints, most hid in the tombs of time. Before the influx of organized and politically based religions, winds were part of everyday life in many cultures. Roman farmers had personal gods for every occasion—for example, calling upon Cardea to open and close doors. The Japanese would call upon the cleansing breath of Fūjin to clear the path. The Latvian wind mother Veja Mate provides nourishment. Each of the 29 winds deities detailed in Part IV of this book has a different role to play, and can help you deepen and enhance your connection with nature.

The east, south, west, and north cardinal winds provide structure for humanity by providing spatial guidance for navigating Earth. The 29 inner winds intersect with the space to provide timeline guidance and individual experience.

While they are not here to work strictly on your behalf, the wind gods and goddesses will assist you when called. It is your job to walk in the open air and listen for their messages. Messages can be as subtle as the rustling of leaves on trees, or fierce enough to grab your full attention. Global winds can disrupt the status quo of an entire country. The winds in this book will guide you through thick and thin, if you take time to listen to their messages.

Dealing with Loss and Grief: There are times in life when grief is unbearable. When you lose a child or loved one, the grieving process takes time. In the Mapuchi tribe of Chile, widows wear black for a full year as a sign of loss and mourning. Lakota people offer a *wopila* feast a year after a loved one's spirit takes wind flight from the physical body. People with a deep connection to the land understand that healing grief is like cultivating a crop; it takes a full season or more to heal. During the dark days of a northern winter, cold winds blow. This is the time to retreat—to rest, tell stories, and stay warm by the fire. In Western culture, we are not equipped to hold a safe space for grief, pain, or suffering. Often, we selfishly try to coax people out of the cycle of grief in order to make ourselves feel better. The greatest gift you can give someone who has lost a precious love is to become like the Dogoda, the steady Polish wind of compassion, and allow them that space to feel their loss.

The more tuned in you become with nature, the more aware you become of your grief process. One mother, blinded by grief after losing her child, pushed everyone away in anger. She left her beloved community garden untended, growing weeds of disappointment with her tears. There was a point when friends stopped coming to share time in the garden, and left her alone to suffer. Eventually, she surrendered to her grief and the healing winds began to stir. Her healing process began by planting small containers of vegetables on her patio. Nature is a persistent healer and friend. Another friend who lost her life partner to breast cancer texted all her friends as she approached her first holiday alone, soon after her partner's death: "I am going inward on a silent retreat." I responded, "I am here, a witness to your process."

A shaman friend who is deeply connected to the earth shares her story of offering grief to the wind. Her life partner died during winter. She would wrap up and sit outside in their medicine wheel, let the winds take her into the deep cold, and she would howl along with them. "I would give them my grief, rage, and heartbreak—give them my denial, my bargaining, my disbelief, my sorrow, and my broken heart. The winds wrapped around me, rocking me fiercely. This hard embrace pressed all over my body, holding me tight, keeping me in my body, in the experience. It kept me grounded and present when all I wanted was to flee."[2] This is a testament to the healing powers of nature and wind.

As the grief process continues over time, the winds of new beginnings stir in the east. As the light returns, grief begins to diminish. A person with a healthy mind will gradually emerge from their darkness and slowly reenter the stream of life. As they move forward in a southerly direction, emotional winds will beckon and true emotional weeding will commence, as unhealed emotions do not get buried with your loved one. As the cycle comes full circle, the loss is woven into the fabric of life.

Grief allows us to hold our parent, lover, friend, addiction, or animal until we are ready to let go. For me, pictures of a beloved pet once triggered memories of past behaviors and energy patterns. The early loss of my father showed me that after death, we still have a relationship. I create new stories that include him. One of my favorite memories is of visiting his grave on his birthday, sharing my success and my sadness that he never got to interact with my healed self.

Heartbreak: Ilmarinen, the Finnish wind god, lost his beloved bride. Bereft, he decided to forge a new lover, made of gold and silver. However, his magical powers were unable to bring this statue to life, because it was void of wind energy. The object had little worldly value and its very presence cut Ilmarinen like a knife, a constant reminder of his loss.

Heartbreak robs people of the present moment. Every experience in life counts; the healing process makes us wiser. After I quit drinking, it took years to rediscover joy. The journey required dancing with the bear of depression. For years, I stumbled in the darkness without a flashlight. One day, a wise teacher recommended a swami who could heal my heartbreak, the cause of my lingering melancholy. Desperate for any wind that could sweep away those darkened hopeless days, I decided to visit this saint. After I followed his prescribed dose of daily mantras, the light of hope ignited and the winds began to stir.

Savor each day of this cycle, as there will come a day when you will miss your depression and sadness. Days spent languishing in pity will be replaced by a busy life. You will need to establish working boundaries and self-care as "time-outs" become a choice, not a sentence.

Wind work will help. About a year after the *shaktipa* with the swami, I noticed I was no longer sourcing from a place of pain. When you are struggling with powerful forces of light and shadow in your soul, call upon Vedic wind god Vayu to help you surrender. Deep wounds leave vibrant scars, which can become treasured assets.

Staying in the Present Moment: Wind always blows in the present moment. The desert nomads of ancient Turkey were wind believers known as Yörük. When faced with a simoom (a powerful, hot, dusty storm) from the wind mother Yel Ana, they would take cover under strategically placed tarps, and patiently wait out the storm. It is hard to stay focused when the winds of change are blowing. Illness, death, jobs, loss—and even joyous events like book publishing, childbirth, or love—create an ever-changing landscape of shifting sand. Staying present with the process is key when whipping winds are raging, as mindfulness creates the space for change.

Sand dunes can move a city block during a storm. The only way to find your way back home is to become highly attuned to the signposts, such as the location of the mound, direction of the wind, or the position of the sun, moon, and stars. Desert dwellers know that dunes form at ninety-degree angles to the prevailing wind, so if the wind blows in from the east, the dunes will run north to south.[3] Are you aware of the subtleties in your own landscape? Presence will help you safely navigate any storm. A familiar nightly walk can become your ally and teacher.

To stay present, you must also learn to let go. You cannot hold the wind in your hand. This concept is valuable for renouncing people, places, and situations that are beyond your control. When plagued by obsessive or churning thoughts, I imagine placing them into a hot air balloon and releasing them to the wind. This simple exercise, when repeated, helps my clients and me to remain present. It is important to remain focused on the current task at hand. After a storm, you may need to regroup, pick up debris, and even rebuild. Just remember that you can build a stronger structure or change its location, but you cannot predict how it will weather the next storm. Preparation and planning are a good use of time. However, worrying is like sweeping the patio in a dust storm: a futile waste of time.

A daily routine is helpful to remain present. As a former chef, my daily routine once included chopping onions, peeling garlic, and setting up the *mis-en-place* (putting things in place). The very act of cooking kept me present and grounded in my body, even as gale-force winds swirled around me.

Find the one thing you love to do, and do it well! Call upon the appropriate wind to help you get moving. Oyá is great when you need to eliminate your "yeah, buts." Wind goddess Yoruba will cut right through your delusions and get you back on track.

Pause and reflect when everything seems to move too quickly around you. Nature provides us with rest points in eternity, gaps between things, events, and cycles. These are places of presence. While performing a vision quest for three days and three nights on the mountain, I experienced firsthand the earth's pause. There was a fleeting moment when time stood still and the day reset itself. Wind gods/goddesses know this time/space gap well. Sila Innua is the indwelling spirit of all things for the Netsilik Inuit. Before responding to the elements of weather, hunting, or name-giving, the indigenous ones connect to the soul of the snow, caribou, or place, before taking any action. One time a wise woman said to me, "Renee, you can sit on the curb for ten years and your destiny will find you." Fifteen years later, I was minding my own business when the phone rang. The call came from a spa keeper who had heard that I was a shaman. She offered me a job that launched my destined work as a soul coach.

As you explore these winds of presence, you can simultaneously engage in activities such as meditation, running marathons, skiing, gardening, cooking, weaving, coloring, singing, walking in the woods, journaling, etc., and remain grounded.

Changing Direction: Once you align to the forces of nature, you become attuned to your natural surroundings. Lapp reindeer herders are keenly aware that survival on barren ice is dependent upon paying attention to the subtle clues of nature, especially knowing when to change direction. When Bieg-Olmai (The Wind Man) arrives as a strong headwind, reindeer retreat. Awareness of wind patterns has helped these people survive by aiding them in knowing when to alter their course.

It is not always in your best interest to charge forward. People often change jobs, houses, and partners, without considering the consequences of their actions. Although the salary may be better at a new job, relationships with workmates could be tenuous. During housing booms, you may secure a property only to feel stranded without financial support when the market course corrects and the property value plummets. When strong winds blow on a relationship, you may leave only to find yourself in the same windstorm with someone new.

Early explorers learned to minimize the risk of travel by first heading into the prevailing wind on outward, exploratory journeys, allowing for safe return by using the force of wind at their backs.[4] You can do the same in your life. A child first learns to walk by holding on to objects within grasp. When a client is stuck in a "no-wind situation" and unable to move forward, my suggestion is to take baby steps in any direction. It will become immediately apparent if the wind supports your forward movement. Cooperating with the wind allows you to adjust, compensate, and make course corrections as needed.

Go with the Flow: Norse sailors from the first century AD were explorers who understood wind patterns. At first, many Viking ships were blown off course. After several failed attempts, the explorers learned how to work with the winds and navigate the seas safely. Call upon Norse god Njord when you need wind power to reach your destination.

Learning to work with wind energy makes good economic and spiritual sense. Since all elements in life are interconnected, a change in wind direction, speed, and intensity will affect how much energy is expended. For instance, riding a bicycle uphill against the wind requires more time and energy than riding downhill with a steady wind at your back. Acknowledging the wind patterns in your life presents options: you can change your direction, wait for shifting winds, or continue to move forward. A disagreement may lead to an argument, which is a waste of energy; but if you wait for the winds to shift, your perspective will change. Advice I once offered to an angry client about timing led to the following response: "Renee, tomorrow it will not matter." Precisely.

There will always be unexpected surprises and obstacles in your life's path. Shifting winds offer clues on how to move beyond these hurdles. As you work with these energies, you learn to retreat, take responsibility, and move forward with confidence, knowing that a favorable wind is at your back.

Personal Gods: Prayer did not begin inside a church. Long before there were houses of worship, peasants gathered stones in the fields and created sacred circles in the forest. Gods were plentiful and personal. When I discovered the winds of spirit, my deepest wound became my greatest strength. For the first time in my life, no matter what I faced, I knew the winds had my back.

The day I received a cherished publishing contract for this book, I plummeted into a sad heart; there was a lingering worry that I would be described as a "fraud." I took a walk—for me, a meditative practice. As I strolled along, I was embraced by a gentle breeze that whispered in my ears, "We have you." In the moment, I embodied the wind and knew what our ancestors knew about nature. For the first time in my life, I had a cooperating relationship with a personal god. The winds had my back.

As you walk with the winds of spirit, you will discover that they can help you develop a naturally evolving organic relationship with the energetic forces in your life, as you navigate safely toward your intended harbor. In Chapter 3, you will be introduced to basic meteorology that will help you develop your skills of observation. Increasing your wind knowledge can help you navigate change no matter what winds are brewing. As you become familiar with these forces of nature, you can start to call on them for help and as cooperating forces of energy in your life.

Randomly open any page in Part IV of this book whenever you need support. As you become familiar with their unique energy, you can summon a wind god/goddess of your own choosing for healing. Call in Basque wind mother Mari when you feel lost. Invite wind god Tȟaté to send you a message. Beckon the Polish wind god of compassion to comfort you. Healing takes time. Use your grief to connect more deeply with Mother Nature.

CHAPTER 3

INTENSITY:
TYPES OF WIND

*"Of all the forces of nature, I should think the wind
contains the largest amount of motive power—
that is, power to move things."*[1]

— ABRAHAM LINCOLN

Life is a passionate adventure, and once you master the
basics skills of navigation, the divine force of wind will propel
you toward your awakening. A skilled sailor can master a ship's
lines and sails, but wisdom is required to navigate the sea successfully. By acknowledging the divine presence of wind, you engage
"nature consciousness" in your life as an invaluable tool for navigating change.

Sailboats are equipped with rudders for steering, and center-
boards to maintain balance. As you work with the processes of
wind work (discussed in Part III of this book) you will strengthen
your ability to steer and stay on course. The qualities of surrender,
acceptance, devotion, forgiveness, and mindfulness comprise your
centerboard; once honed, these qualities will keep you steady in
rough waters. Mastering these tools will help you assuredly raise
your sail to catch the winds of life.

THE POWER OF WIND

Wind is an emanating force of nature, the bulk movement of air along the surface of the planet. Life on our planet cannot survive without wind. Likewise, as your inner winds begin to stir, you are propelled forward through life.

If there were no winds, disaster would soon follow: the planet would heat up; scum would cover rivers, lakes, and oceans; fish would die; crops would fail, and people would starve. All life on planet Earth begins and ends with wind (breath). It is time to rekindle your friendship with the elements of nature, especially the wind. Wind provides you with a direct intimate connection to spirit. The best way to live in a state of harmony is to feed your soul the divine energy of wind.

Meteorologists measure wind by strength and direction. As you wake up to wind power, you will begin to understand how energy influences your life. Wind affects the movement of your ongoing life cycles through space and time. Crosswinds can intersect one's path and slow down forward motion. Storm squalls wreak havoc. Euphoria may arrive on the wings of a soaring eagle. Becalmed, your ship may be stranded midsea. As you begin to observe wind patterns in your life, you will become familiar with forces that contribute to your range of experience.

Force—Pressure: A sail pulls the boat forward in the same way that a wing lifts an airplane. The aerodynamic forces of wind on the sail, combined with the rudder and centerboard in the water below, propel the boat forward. Wind is simple yet complex. The wind flowing from a high-pressure zone of the sail into a lower pressure area of water is known as gradient force. Wind always seeks the path of least resistance.

Like wind, energy naturally moves from areas of high density to places of low density. An unconscious person is like a vacuum, capable of drawing energy from a person who is awake. If you are unaware of how these forces work in your life, you may unknowingly lift and propel other people forward, while decreasing your own wind power. Be on the lookout for people or situations that drain your energy and hinder your awakening.

As you inhale, air is heated. It then expands as it fills your lungs, which causes you to exhale. This breath wind connects you to everything. As you expand your human capacity through awakening, your spiritual energy becomes a pressurized force of nature, a wind of peace manifested outward as a service to others. This cycle continues until you reach the end of your life and exhale your final breath.

Patterns—Coriolis Force: Nature consists of repeating cycles. Just as the Earth revolves around the sun, your life moves in cyclical patterns of experience. Every day you wake up and follow your routine, day in and day out, while the years pass by. If the Earth did not rotate at an angle, wind would move in a straight line. The same is true in your life; each growth cycle creates new responses.

In my early career, job cycles always ended abruptly due to a personality clash. Eventually, I became an employee who could navigate the system by getting along with others. The work cycle is patterned in nature with a beginning, middle, and end. Leaving to pursue a dream creates a new legacy. From a superior ending, you create a new jumping-off point for the next cycle.

Today's experiences differ from those of the past. Imagine your body as a ship that crosses wind's path. You need to adjust your heading to account for wind patterns and currents, or you could get caught in a gyres (spiral). Navigating effectively and staying the course requires constant adjustment.

The stronger the wind, the more difficult it is to stay on track. Imagine yourself changing a significant pattern in your life, such as overcoming an addiction. As you begin to awaken, you become aware that ingesting alcohol changes your mood and takes you off course. Yet, after eliminating alcohol from your life, you get depressed. This catch-22 scenario either takes you off course and back toward your addiction, or leads toward surrender and a stronger flight plan such as therapy, church, 12-step meetings, or treatment. These winds of grace can bring you to your knees. Learning from experience can make you a better sailor. The goal of the awakened traveler is to observe, reflect, and move forward with ease.

Friction: Learning to work with wind energy makes good economic and spiritual sense. Since all elements in life are interconnected, a change in wind direction, speed, and intensity will affect how much energy is expended. For instance, tacking against the wind requires more time and energy than sailing with a steady wind at your back. Acknowledging wind patterns in your life provides options: you can change direction, wait for shifting winds, or continue to move forward. A disagreement may lead to an argument, which is a waste of energy. If you wait for the winds to shift, your perspective will change. The advice I offered to an angry client about timing led to the following response: "Renee, tomorrow it will not matter." Precisely.

Working with your winds is the best way to reach your destination. For example, it may be your job to care for an aging parent, but this responsibility might clip your wings and prevent you from advancing your own projects. Alternatively, caring for your mother could provide the impetus for a long-awaited healing. Like a branch on a tree, you will learn to bend in the storm. When the timing is right, you will move forward.

WIND INTENSITY:
ENERGY HAS DIFFERENT INTENSITIES

> *Rock–a–bye baby, on the treetop,*
> *When the wind blows, the cradle will rock,*
> *When the bough breaks, the cradle will fall,*
> *And down will come baby, cradle and all.* [2]

There comes a time in each person's life when torrential winds wreak havoc and everything falls apart. Yet it is from such experiences that a solid foundation can be built. For example, in the aftermath of several California earthquakes, city bylaws were established that required buildings to be retrofitted to withstand intense movement. Are you prepared for unseen windstorms in your life?

The correlation between wind and energy is abstract, as both are invisible forces, yet they demonstrate visible effects in your life. A tree branch tapping your window at night might wake you up, as will the subtle winds of spirit. Attune yourself by calling upon these forces of spirit to elevate your level of service. Gifts of the experience of calling upon wind energy are: clear thinking, happiness, improved relationships, health, and wellness.

Wind is a fluctuating force of nature. Variations of wind speed and intensity can come from within, in the form of your prevailing beliefs and ideas, needs and emotions, physical body and endings, spiritual beliefs, and community. They can also take the form of external forces of nature. It is prudent to become aware of wind intensity. The awakened person flows with shifting winds and will see the fruit ripening on the distant tree. Keep in mind that on any given day, you may encounter one of the following.

Tailwind: A tailwind blows favorably in your current direction of travel. Working with a tailwind can help you achieve a goal quickly. The ancient practice of tying wind knots (which we will discuss in Chapter 14) can be used to harness wind power, which can then be released as needed. One wind believer (a practitioner of wind work) released some stored energy when she needed an influx of money; that same day she signed up two new clients. External tailwinds might, for instance, manifest as snowfall at a ski resort, which in turn provides tourists to support your business.

Headwind: A headwind blows against you. While we often think of opposition as a negative force, keep in mind that kites and airplane use this aerodynamic for lift. When sailing at sea, this opposing force is overcome by tacking. As you learn to maneuverer your way around oncoming winds, there is the potential to build internal strength and wisdom. At the age of 40, I received a message that my cat was about to pass away. That night, when I returned home from work, Dash was nowhere to be found. This wind came headlong into my life, causing a period of deep depression. During the healing process, I changed jobs, took a class on shamanism, and adjusted my sails toward my awaiting destiny.

Political opposition can become a headwind as well. The 2016 United States presidential election caused an evolutionary swell in people paying attention to world politics. Staying on course during those stormy times was a challenge for most. Once people got their bearings, mass discontent created a groundswell of energy directed at planetary concerns. Thousands of people gathered at Standing Rock in North Dakota to protest the drilling of a pipeline underneath the Missouri River. Strong headwinds create the needed lift for these water protectors, just as it does planes, kites, and large gatherings standing for a common cause. Learning to use these forces of nature will help you gather speed and strength as you begin to trust you.

Crosswind: This refers to when the wind is moving perpendicular to your course of action. Winds naturally move north and south, yet due to the Earth's rotation, and other obstacles such as water, mountains, forests, and buildings, wind gets deflected. This force of energy can be used to your advantage. Sailors learn to tack back and forth. Detours to your goal may bear many gifts. When you least expect it, you might receive a windfall of money. This is a positive side wind. For instance, traffic tickets might come as side winds, slowing you down, but this ten-minute distraction could help you avoid a car accident. Learning to move with shifting winds is always for your benefit.

Gales: When these very strong winds move with or against you, it may indicate that you need some support. For example, a marriage had capsized when a couple decided to make a major cross-country move. Up until this time, they had shared interests and their home life had been stable. However, as the hurricane-force winds blew hard, each partner needed to self-evaluate and decided to seek counseling to steady their relationship. There are times when strong winds are required to enrich your experience. After the experience, the couple began to explore separate activities that made them happy. The power shifted dramatically.

Intermittent winds are unreliable, unpredictable, and not always available when you need energy. Such sporadic winds are independent forces of nature that are beyond your control. Their strength varies throughout the day; in nature, wind is strongest at night and early morning. Despite their changeable nature, you can learn to work with these scattered winds. Some writers find that the wee hours of the morning are the best time to tap into energy of concentrated wind. Still, there are times when these fickle winds stall. Awareness of your own wind patterns will allow you to adjust, compensate, and stay on course.

Doldrums is a nautical term used to describe areas in the Pacific and Atlantic Oceans along the equator, where the prevailing winds are calm to nonexistent—a place of inactivity. During times when the wind ceases to blow in your life, you will need to stop. For instance, a runner who breaks her right foot is forced to stop and perhaps examine her beliefs about moving forward. When the wind ceases to blow below the equator, sailors pinpoint their location using the Southern Cross instead of the wind. Likewise, when your forward activity is blocked, you may need additional tools and support to stay afloat as you wait for the winds to shift.

Within every being resides a divine, serene place. The Buddhists call this state *nirvana*, which literally translates as "no wind." In the human state of consciousness, it is impossible to live in constant bliss. Temporary states of euphoria can only be accessed under certain conditions such as meditation, shamanic journeys, marathons, and while gazing deeply into the eyes of your beloved. *Nirvana* is an invisible inspiration; a gentle, peaceful wind that can carry you across the threshold into lofty worlds of unlimited possibilities. The key to achieving bliss is to weave these invisible threads of possibility into down-to-earth, real-life experiences. This is a very special state where hard work and magic meld into a perfect union. Tapping into the sublime energy of these divine winds allows you to enter into a state of gratitude, presence, and divine wisdom.

While *nirvana* is an expansive experience, a contracted state of "no wind" also exists. Polynesian legend speaks of a time when a conniving Captain Cook character landed on their island. When it was realized that Captain Cook was not the beneficial god of agriculture that their myths had prophesied, the natives coined the word *haole*, which translates to "no wind" in English, to describe Caucasian foreigners who had no spirit. White people brought disruptive energies that destroyed the natives' peaceful existence.

To better understand the meaning of wind intensity, imagine a circle in which the energy of stagnation (no spirit), *haole*, is at the 1-degree mark, while the energy of *nirvana* is at the 359-degree mark. Along the perimeter of this circle lies a spectrum of ever-increasing wind intensity, starting as a static "no wind," rising up incrementally to a gale-force storm, and then back down to the 1-degree mark.

These powerful forces intersect your life on a daily basis. When your umbilical cord is cut at birth, you leave behind your borrowed breath and your life begins. In between life and death, there will be times of no wind, while at other times you will need to stand firm and hold on to your hat.

INNER WINDS

Where did wind consciousness gain recognition? A popular scientific theory is that a major comet struck Earth between 12,800 and 11,600 years ago, bringing an abrupt end to global warming.[3] Wind gods/goddesses appeared on the scene approximately 10,600 years ago. Many creation myths from this period speak of a time when the Earth was covered by water, which later receded. For example, the Ojibwa legend known as the Long-Tailed Heavenly Climbing Star speaks of a cataclysmic star that changed the Earth.[4] Heat melted the northern ice sheets, causing global flooding, which brought about rapid cooling. The ice age of the Younger Dryas lasted approximately 1,300 years and caused major extinction across the globe. A dense layer of debris covered the Earth, until the winds began to stir.

Mystics often speak of inner feuding and the manipulation of power as the cause of the demise of former civilizations. Does history repeat itself? Here we are again, at a similar junction of global warming, with ice caps breaking apart. I believe these wind gods/goddesses have now appeared as teachers, providing humanity with wisdom and an opportunity to restore balance in the world.

The inner wind gods/goddesses initially appeared as a creative consciousness that worked in harmony with the sun god to restore life on the planet as floods receded. That is why it is so crucial for us to tap into our divinity, and remember that we are connected to the Earth and shifting winds. Learning to work with these conscious winds will help you heal and show you how to walk upon Mother Earth in a dignified manner.

GLOBAL WINDS

A breeze from the Pacific Northwest can circumnavigate the world in a few days, an ever-important reminder that we are all connected through the wind.

One time in Peru, the Q'ero were reading cocoa leaves as part of a divination into world affairs. The patterns in the leaves suggested that viruses would become rampant, propagated, and carried by wind. This prediction is coming true. In one study, Kawasaki disease, a leading cause of heart defects in children under five worldwide, has been found to be carried by a regional wind from northeast China to Japan.[5] Other airborne soil-related bacteria and fungi are now being studied. Diseases like the West Nile Virus are being propagated around the globe by airborne mosquitos. Perhaps this has always been the way of the world. Social media websites such as Facebook, Instagram, and Twitter provide regular warnings of such epidemics, but also engender fear as pathogens get carried across the globe by the wind.

Not all winds come with forewarning. Abrupt tsunamis, earthquakes, and tropical storms alter landscapes forever. Man-made "winds" like murder and terrorism strike unexpectedly. Both types of wind have global impacts and can change life in an instant. This is not a dualistic idea of good or bad, right or wrong. Our actions directly impact the outcome of life on planet Earth.

The ideas of good (virtue) and bad (sin) as ethical determinants did not exist in early indigenous cultures. Each culture had a netherworld (underworld) to receive the dead, but it was not a place of punishment. Hell was the later invention of religion. In nature, however, conflicting energies have always existed. A delightful summer breeze could bring welcome rain, or rush in as a violent tornado that destroys property and ruins crops. Outraged over the noise and overpopulation, Sumerian god Enlil is said to have annihilated an entire civilization. When out of harmony with nature, Scandinavian wind spirit Bieg-Olmai would deprive fishermen of bountiful catches. Annual celebrations and ceremonies were created to appease and honor these wind deities. To this day, every February in Korea, worshippers offer food to appease Yeongdeung Halmang; they believe that if they feed her rice cakes, she will be unable to blow forcefully and destroy their rice fields.

Life on our planet is dependent upon individuals taking collective action. Two thousand individuals with a laser-point global focus stood together to protect water along the Missouri River. Peaceful protesters had the wind at their backs as they prayed to stop the fossil fuel industry giants from boring under the river. To heal destructive winds battering our humanity, it is imperative to do your own personal healing. Once you harmonize with your inner winds, you will be available for a cooperating relationship with Mother Earth. While wind will shake you, truth will become fixed, like the North Star in the night sky.

With each awakened step that you take, you become a curious onlooker of your own experience. Exploring life's precious moments as a mystery to be savored, you will begin to recognize the wind patterns described in Chapter 4. Cooperating with these forces of nature prepares you to strategize and safely navigate to your intended harbor. Even when you get caught off guard in a storm, you will be able to quickly change direction, without losing your bearings.

CHAPTER 4

RECOGNIZING
WIND PATTERNS:
CYCLES OF CHANGE

*"There is no good in arguing with the inevitable.
The only argument available with an east wind is
to put on your overcoat."*

— JAMES RUSSELL LOWELL

Long before the Weather Channel, along with observation, direct experience, and folklore, many tools were available to predict the changing patterns of nature. For your own direct experience, go outside, close your eyes, and slowly spin clockwise until you feel the air moving across your face. If you are by a lake, you can observe how the wind causes small ripples to form on the water's surface. You can also watch swaying flags, weather vanes, smoke, moving branches, or scurrying leaves.

Windward is the word used to describe the direction the wind blows: from the north, east, south, or west. Interpreting signs from directional (cardinal) winds is a useful skill. Winds at your back allow you to move forward with grace and ease, while headwinds can cause delay, frustration, and stagnation. The awakened sailor remembers that both windward and headwinds are part of the experience.

First-century Sufi poets held that no matter what your challenge, "This too shall pass."[2] You only need to wait a few hours, days, months, or years, and the winds will shift. Fortunately, human beings are resilient and adaptable. Humanity currently finds itself on the threshold of a new grand cycle, in the same way that our planet cycles through her seasons. Spring always blows in with winds that shake apart the winter landscape.

AWAKENING TO THE WIND OF CHANGE

Understanding cardinal wind themes can help you forecast from your present moment experience. Experience is universal and cyclical, like nature. The inner winds of spirit individualize your experience, making your cycle unique. These inner winds of spirit may be called upon for help and guidance. By contrast, global winds affect world affairs. These powerful energies represent the positive and negative polarity of planet Earth. They are the winds of change that can provide the impetus for people to awaken, be self-sufficient, and minimize their carbon footprint. Yet these winds also carry airborne illnesses and pollution that can lead to global destabilization. Waking up allows you to understand and cooperate with all types of wind. Healing the earth begins by healing oneself.

MANAGING DAILY CHANGE

On any given day, one or more inner winds may stir as you cycle through your life. It is important to know where and how they intersect your thoughts, feelings, body, or spirit. They might appear as gentle breezes, a tropical storm, or a short hard blast of cold air. Remember that you can restart your day at any point you choose. You might wake up to a thunderous wind in the east, but by suppertime you could be enjoying a friendly breeze blowing in from the west.

As you traverse through the day, you will intersect with others, and depending on how the winds are blowing in your life, relationships may or may not take form. Using your gut responses and intuition to understand your cardinal winds will give you a better understanding of why people come and go.

There are several possibilities and options when approaching a checkout stand at a store. When you are aligned with the wind at your back, a checker opens up an additional cash register line and sends you through first. Or you could get caught in a deceptive crosswind of second-guessing the cashiers and lane changing, which then delays your departure. Once you start paying attention to your natural inner wisdom and are able to bend with the wind, you will discover valuable lessons in both experiences. Spending more time in the store might be just what you need to avoid a detour.

THE LANDSCAPE OF CHANGE

Pre-Columbian Indians in Peru divided their landscape into sections, and built roads and cities based on cardinal wind directions. The famed Inca Trail, part of The Qhapaq Ñan (Great Inca Road or the beautiful road), runs north to south, outward from Cuzco (the navel). For these people, each of the four directions— east, south, west, north—offered distinct resources. Most major roads and highways are still oriented to the cardinal compass point directions, mirroring the cosmic setup of planets and stars in the heavens.

Your life is also divided in four directions of experience. Navigation is experience dependent; every action creates a new opportunity. Everything new has a foundation in what came before. Your spiritual magnetic north is always relative to your current situation and location. Think of your life as an island, a collection of personal experiences that stretches as far as your imagination; this is your personal map. You cannot navigate from yesterday, or tomorrow, in the same way that you cannot adjust your coordinates from France when you live in the United States. The wind always blows in the present.

Unlike cartographers who relied on the early navigators to map the world, you must take on the roles of both navigator and cartographer and create your own map. In the early days of sailing, aside from learning the ropes and sails, sailors learned to orient themselves from the helm of the ship by learning the 32 points on the compass card, a rotating card indicating the 32 key bearings (wind points). As magnetics were applied to orientation, the compass rose became the standard tool for navigation. Further markers on the magnetic compass divide the 360 points around the circumference of the circular card into quarters, denoting the four cardinal directions and intermediate points. To get from point 0 to point 360 requires many stops along the way. By removing resistance at each point along the perimeter, you can catch the winds of grace in your sail and move forward, or reposition your rudder to shift course.

Spiritual
Community
Germinating

Physical Body
Endings
Harvest

Mind
Ideas
New Beginning

Needs
Emotions
Tending

This tracking system can be applied to your life; the cardinal winds symbolize the thematic cycles of experience: east represents the mind; south, the emotions; west, the physical; and north represents the spiritual. (Chapter 11 in Part III provides step-by-step instructions for determining which wind you are currently facing.) The intercardinal points on the compass card represent the subtle shifts from one point to the next in any given cycle of time. While traveling the road from the spiritual territory of the north, to a new beginning in the east, you will experience subtle or dramatic shifts such as hibernation, renewal, and inspiration. It is important to call upon the wind gods and goddesses, to teach you how to navigate safely through each point along your journey.

Today's navigational systems are mostly computerized. Global positioning technology can be accessed remotely via wireless communications from satellites orbiting the planet. Yet, although it is easy to pinpoint the location of people and objects with incredible precision, it still takes firsthand experience and a compass to be an adept sailor. A sailor needs to understand the movements of tides, currents, winds, celestial bodies, and topography to reach his destination. Similarly, being aware of your inner compass and in tune with the winds will help you to make better decisions as you navigate through life.

As you orient to life using your body's signals, you will become more receptive to the messages generated by your internal navigational system. Imagine that your body is a compass needle providing you with all the information needed to chart a course of equanimity and purpose. As you awaken and become observer to your emotions and physical sensations, you will learn to navigate safely through life no matter which way the wind(s) may be blowing.

HOW DO YOU KNOW WHEN YOU ARE OFF COURSE?

My afflictions belong to me and my art—they have become one with me. Without illness and anxiety, I would have been a rudderless ship.[3]

— EDVARD MUNCH

Just like the pioneer sea captains who set out to explore and map the world, you may also become lost and disoriented. Aligning to the winds of spirit will enable you to navigate through life successfully, no matter which way the forces of nature are moving.

You will become like a homing pigeon that uses the earth's magnetism to find its way home.

Consider your physical body as a luxury yacht piloted by your spiritual self, as it cruises the waterways of your life. To achieve optimal performance, scheduled maintenance is required. Severe pain, obesity, anorexia, life-threatening illnesses, chronic ailments, insomnia, and broken bones are indicators that your compass may be out of alignment. These negative states are headwinds forcing you back toward the shore, where you can find respite from sailing in whichever waters are causing you distress.

Being off course does not mean you are doing something wrong or bad. Detours can be valuable guideposts leading to an expansion of consciousness. One time I was so heartbroken that I used magic to bring back my beloved. I learned that while sorcery can be effective in attaining a desired result, the outcome is not always in my best interest. As it turned out, getting lost at sea was the best way for me to learn about the consequences of making poor choices. As a healer, it is essential to understand both the bright and shadowy aspects of life. If I can save a client a journey to the gallows, then my years of torment spent lost at sea, without a compass, were worth it.

Feelings fall into two main categories. The first category includes positive feelings we have when our needs are met. The "Feelings and Needs" sheet produced by the Center for Nonviolent Communication states that these are feelings of affection, confidence, gratitude, serenity, engagement, inspiration, joy, hope, and exhilaration.[4] The second category, when our needs are not met, is composed of negative feelings such as fear, confusion, embarrassment, tension, annoyance, loneliness, pain, anger, addiction, and despair.

Children are resilient: when they fall off a swing, they howl and scream, but moments later all is forgotten and they're back on the swing full of gusto. However, society frowns upon adults who express their emotions and throw tantrums. As a result, their feelings are driven underground. This is more likely to happen to those who grew up in families that discouraged the sharing of feelings. Adults who have survived abuse, addiction, and violence in childhood tend to bury and hide their emotions. Consequently, the wind will shake leaves from the branches, leaving such people with mood disorders or physical diseases. Without warning, Zephyrus, the chilling autumn wind, scatters the leaves from your past into your present life. If this happens, remember that your body is a fine-tuned instrument that can help you navigate through life's trials and tribulations. Once you begin the process of waking up, you will realize that although pain is inevitable, suffering is optional.

TOOLS ARE USEFUL ONLY WHEN APPLIED

If you are lost in the woods and your compass is tucked away in your backpack, it serves no purpose whatsoever; you must use it to find your way home. Similarly, reading this book might be a great beginning toward unpacking your compass, but results require action. Your emotions are like the compass in your backpack; even though you are not paying attention to it, the needle still seeks to point north. You must pull out the compass, focus your attention, and apply your skills if you truly desire to get back home safe and sound.

As long as you are alive, the winds will continue to blow. They can either disrupt or soothe you. When the wind blows, your task in awakening is to learn to sway and bend like a willow tree, rather than break.

PUTTING IT ALL TOGETHER

The pieces of the wind puzzle are beginning to fit together. The goal of Part I is to teach you how to cooperate with the winds and awaken your divine nature. The cycle of awakening moves you from basic awareness to a true spiritual awakening, which provides a personal direct divine experience. Over time you will experience a radical shift of consciousness, from which you can never fully retreat again. Awakening is a journey, and every experience leaves a mark on your life, a higher perspective, a jumping-off place from which you can build upon. You will discover how to tap into the powerful forces of nature for guidance, and know when to plant, weed, grow, harvest, and rest. Nature will provide the map. Your work is to be ever present and become a conscious observer.

The following section describes the cardinal winds, which provide thematic guidance for your experience. The cardinal winds are integral dynamic forces of nature that have shaped human consciousness by providing universal structure to order experience. Hunters and gatherers had a polished honing system in the pineal gland of their brain, shown by their ability to migrate back and forth from established seasonal locations. Over time they devised simple line maps for guidance based on these compass card cardinal wind directions. Sailors used magnetic compasses to navigate the seas based on the forces of nature. You cannot reach a destination if you plot your course from the bridge of someone else's ship; you must determine your own location if you want to navigate through life successfully.

Part II

fROM WHAT DIRECTION IS THE WIND BLOWING?

CARDINAL FORCES

THE WINDS OF FATE

One ship drives east and another drives west
With the self-same winds that blow;
'Tis the set of the sails
And not the gales
That tells them the way to go.
Like the winds of the sea are the winds of fate
As we voyage along through life;
'Tis the set of the soul
That decides its goal
And not the calm or the strife.[1]

INTRODUCTION
TO THE CARDINAL
WINDS

A Child Blessing
Turned by the winds goes the one I send yonder;
Yonder he goes who is whirled by the winds;
Goes, where the four hills of life and the four winds are standing;
There, into the midst of the winds do I send him,
Into the midst of the winds, standing there![1]

For eons, the cardinal winds have had the authority of holding up the four quadrants of the sky. The Cardinal Winds—east, south, west, and north—were the principal markers on the sailor's compass card, and later, the navigational magnetic compass rose. Beyond the metaphor, these energetic wind patterns are the foundation for ordering experience, and are useful for navigating change. These winds represent the mental, emotional, physical, and spiritual territories of your inner and outer landscape. Successfully navigating change requires a deeper understanding of your personal environment. Conscious engagement with the emanating energy of the cardinal winds will provide you with daily guidance.

From an indigenous viewpoint, your world is comprised of continually moving cycles of time and space; the intersections create experience. Cardinal winds are timeline markers in your cycle of experience. Navigating experience by cooperating with your cardinal winds improves every relationship. With a shift in your perception, the world aligns and you become a captain in the sea of change. For example, a former client of mine was ready to abandon her marriage. However, after focused work with her emotional winds, she was healed, and during this spiritual growth spurt, her partner miraculously changed. With continued application of the lessons outlined in this book, you will understand that nothing is broken, and once you make the appropriate adjustments, the fog lifts, unveiling an ever-present blue sky.

Your life's journey is a kind of compass card in itself. From the Omaha Indians, the rite of a child's blessing above shows the understanding of the native people about the natural cycle of life; the four hills signify childhood, youth, adulthood, and old age. To visualize your life as a compass, draw a large circle, which represents your experiences, on a sheet of paper. Divide the sheet of paper into four quarters. The top of the circle represents the north, the bottom south, the right side east, and the left west. Life and daylight begins in the east. The south is your adolescent phase. As you approach the west, you are positioned equidistant between life and death. Northwest to northeast is the area of your wisdom years, while the north represents the pinnacle of your achievements. The territory from north to east is the return to the earth from which you came, dust that moves freely about in the wind. In cosmologies involving reincarnation, the soul flees the decaying body and is reborn in another physical vessel when the timing is right.

During your life span, you will cycle through each of these cardinal territories daily, weekly, monthly, yearly, and in larger several-year cycles. A seven-year cycle could represent the compass card of a child, a project, job, or relationship. After a child's first cycle of life, they could experience loss; a next-door neighbor could move and break their innocent young heart. This gale-force east wind disruption shakes their secure foundation. At eight, they will begin their second cycle around their compass card, with the wisdom that while friends sometimes move away, causing sadness, new friends can ease the loss.

New projects and relationships begin in the east. Shifts in your ideas or thinking are east winds that propel you toward the southern territory of emotions. Before I opened my first restaurant, people would say it takes five years to break even. Over time, I realized it was because businesses have their own divine cyclical pattern that follows nature. After the opening, my emotional maturity was tested. The west winds offered rigorous physical demands, while the north winds provided the necessary cycle for the community to respond. Without customers, a restaurant cannot succeed. If you do not get the community support in the north, your enterprise will not have the wind power to move through the second cycle.

In ancient Greece, the cardinal winds were represented by four immortal gods, the offspring of Aeolus, the Greek god of the winds: Boreas (north), Eurus (east), Notus (south), and Zephyrus (west). In North America, the Lakota Sioux summon Wioheumpata, the light-bearing wind of the east; Itokaga, the wind of growth and warming; Wiyokpiyata, the winds of completion; and the purifying north wind, Waziyata. In Norse mythology, the Four Stags of Yggdrasill are wind steeds, while the four wind dwarves— Austri, Suðri, Vestri, and Norðri—anchor the sky. In China, the arms and legs of the first inhabitant, Pangu, became the four celestial directions. Japan has four guardians called heavenly kings. The Bible makes several references to the four corners of the earth (Ezekiel 7:2, Isaiah 11:12, and Job 37:3). The Made tribe of Africa treasures a seed that sprouted in the center of the universe and expanded to become the four directions. Every primal culture on this planet has ordered their world based on the quaternal concept of wholeness.

The cardinal winds mark the predominant themes found at any given moment within the cycles of your life. These themes are in constant flux. With a smaller event such as cooking dinner, you can move through all four stages of a cycle in an hour. During the day, you may move through all four directional winds as well. A couple might begin the daily cycle of waking together in the east. Yet one person may experience the inner wind of La'amaomao, an ancestral wind associated with building a strong foundation, while the other may awaken to Sila Innua, the introspective wind. Each wind provides a different perspective. Utilizing these dynamic forces provides a useful tool for navigating the day, together and separately. While your partner may arise and immediately start laying bricks for the day, you may require time for personal reflection.

With this in mind, the following four chapters will describe the cardinal winds and how they impact the four sacred areas of your life: the physical body, emotions, beliefs, and spirit.

CHAPTER 5

THE CARDINAL WIND OF THE EAST (THE MIND)

"It looked just as if the wind blew you here."
"It did," said Mary Poppins briefly.[1]

— P. L. TRAVERS

In every tradition, the east wind is associated with ushering in the morning star and springtime. The sun rises in the east everywhere on the planet, and so it is with your life; the east wind is the source of all beginnings. In literature, the east wind is often perceived as a strong disruptive force of nature. In the classic P. L. Travers book *Mary Poppins*, the east wind lifts the nanny up and flings her at the house, announcing her arrival with a "terrific bang."[2] In your life, change can be ushered in with the same dynamic force of nature; disastrous endings prepare the way for hearty new beginnings.

In many Native American cultures, the dry east wind is associated with the majestic eagle, a powerful symbol representing vision. With its acute eyesight, the eagle can spot a rabbit in a field a mile below. Similarly, our minds are capable of "seeing" our place on the map of life. The Lakota Sioux Indians of North America regard the eagle as a mediator between the physical and spiritual worlds; it is a totem animal said to carry our prayers to heaven. South American shamans also speak of a future time when the eagle, representing the north, and the condor, representing the south, will fly as one, symbolizing an age of unity and shared vision among people of all nations.

In winds of the spirit, the east wind represents different qualities of the mind, such as mental acuity or confusion, ability (or lack thereof) to envision the future and make plans, perception, and discernment. If, according to your compass reading in Chapter 11, you are facing an east wind, it means the given situation involves (or should involve) your mind in some manner. It is time to examine your thoughts and beliefs. For ten years, I operated a holistic healing center to inspire healers to become skilled in the art of business. Many of the providers were unable to earn a suitable living. At the root of their poverty consciousness was the belief that healers didn't deserve to be paid in exchange for services rendered. This assumption was historically rooted in indigenous ideology. There was a time in history when the community tended to the shaman's basic needs. Villages disbanded when people moved to the city, leaving healers stranded. Compensation for their services became dollars instead of chickens. Becoming awake requires constant reexamination of your ideas, thoughts, and beliefs. Thirty years ago, cumbersome phones were left at home on the counter. Today's sleek cell phones are crucial instruments for navigating life. Change is a perpetual wind.

Indigenous people are keenly aware of the lands surrounding their community and the winds that blow from each direction. They understand the growing seasons, know the location of food sources, and demonstrate great respect for the local flora and fauna. However, urban communities are not built upon this model. Urban dwellers habitually visit the same favorite grocery stores, pharmacies, dry cleaners, and so on, which are generally within close proximity to their homes. Winds that blow from the eastern landscape can help you establish positive priorities and become fully awake to your inner landscape in relationship to your outer surroundings. With this awareness comes deeper connection to nature.

With practice, you will be able to navigate your way safely across the eastern slopes of your life, no matter how strong the winds may be blowing. You will soar high like an eagle, developing and sustaining a nonjudgmental, clear vision and sense of purpose as you move through life.

THE MIND

The east symbolizes the intellect and the mind. In the industrial world, our mode of thinking has long been based on the linear principles of logic, whereas indigenous shamans believe everything is possible when we change our relationship with time and space.

For many people, the world of the mind is a mysterious domain. Scientists, physicians, psychologists, mathematicians, philosophers, and religious leaders alike have debated its nature, purpose, and function throughout history. Ask a scientist and a religious leader about the mind, and a debate about free will versus determinism, or creationism versus the theory of evolution, is sure to follow.

Physicians might describe the various ways in which the brain acts as the control center for the entire body; they are taught that the mind is a function of the brain. Yet in the last century, physicists have hypothesized that the mind is part of a divinely inspired dance of the universe on a quantum level. This latter perspective is similar to the shamanic approach, which recognizes that everything, including our minds, is interconnected through a vast web of nature.

The ability to reason helped ancient mariners navigate the oceans of the world. They knew that the new moon rose in the east around noon and set again around midnight (though moonrise changes a little, day by day, they knew exactly what those changes were from year to year), and they could plot their travels accordingly. A new idea is similar to a new moon—it is not fully formed, but contains vast potential and wonderful possibilities. As you explore your eastern territory with the help of the wind gods and goddesses, your reasoning powers will increase dramatically and you will learn how to work effectively with your natural inner rhythms.

According to the Vedic tradition of India, a culture that embraces the concept of reincarnation, imprinted memories from our waking lives, our dreams, daydreams, as well as our past and future lives, are stored in the east. Working with the winds can help you discover and understand these imprints, leading to the restoration of harmony and balance in your life. Being present means leaving the past behind and moving forward.

WHEN THE EAST WIND BLOWS

Whenever you feel the mighty breath of an eastern wind sting-ing your face and buffeting your environment, it signifies that you are about to embark upon a new journey. Accept this opportunity with open arms and a smile on your face. Just as the sun rises in the east, your life also starts anew in the east, not only every day, but with every new project, relationship, or stage of life, with a promise of hope and a sense of purpose and renewal. Take time to reflect on the new possibilities being ushered in by the energy of the storm.

Everything in life is cyclical: the four seasons, the planting of crops, business transactions, relationships, and personal growth. In each blessed moment, there is always an opportunity for posi-tive change. Surrendering to the energy of the east means exam-ining your beliefs. Be at peace with your thoughts and healing will surely follow. Fight a thought and the thought prevails. By surrendering to the east, a thought loses momentum and trans-formation occurs.

Heading into an east wind life is a roaring call to adventure. A true adventure demands an upheaval in the natural order of your life. While the east is associated with light, vision, birth, childhood, intuition, and the untamable, it also demands our full attention, so we must be fully prepared for what lies ahead.

Be mindful when the east wind is blowing. Endings followed by new beginnings await you on the horizon. On a small scale, this could mean the arrival of an unexpected visitor, the loss of a job, or a sudden health concern. On a larger scale, it could sig-nify the devastation of communities, nations, and war. From a simple "aha" moment to a major life change, the frontier of the east beckons you to wake up, rise up, and move forward with your senses on alert. Fly high like an eagle and let your indomitable spirit set you free.

CHAPTER 6

THE CARDINAL WIND OF THE SOUTH (THE EMOTIONS)

The south wind . . . when
He had driven me to the house of my lord, I said,
"O South Wind, on the way I shall to thee . . . everything that,
Thy wing, will I break." As he spoke with his mouth,
The wing of the South Wind was broken, seven days
the South Wind blew not upon the land.[1]

Centuries before indigenous storytellers warmed the winter fires and shared tales about the wind that blew from the south to battle with Jack Frost of the north, the Babylonian sage, Adapa encountered the powerful south wind while fishing in the Persian Gulf. According to ancient Sumerian tablets (14th century BCE), Adapa's boat was swallowed when the sea split in two. Enraged by this disruptive event, the fisherman broke the wing of the south wind with his word. For seven days the wind would not blow, ergo Adapa was summoned to heaven to explain his actions. Upon revealing the anger in his heart, Adapa experienced forgiveness. While in heaven, Adapa refused the food and water from the gods that promised everlasting life. Choosing mortal humanity, he was promptly sent back to earth to share his emotional wisdom.[2] The south wind provides a mirror to remind you that words are potent spells that can shift the course of nature and leave everlasting marks on time. Compassion is the gentle wind of pardon.

The strife between human emotion (south wind) and spirit (north wind) has been an enduring theme in mythology. The Cherokee and Hopi peoples refer to this southern wind as the Light Magician, a spirit that ushers in the summer. Hopi legend speaks of a wizard from the north that faces off against a wizard from the south by tossing frozen snowballs into his warm wind. Thus the southern landscape represents youth, innocence, patience, forgiveness, and self-exploration, as well as an opportunity to melt away our emotional problems and move beyond doubts and fears.

The south wind is the fragrant wind of hope and harmony. A new love is a welcome breeze that temporarily clears the air from past disappointment. As new shoots of passion spring forth from the earth, remnants of the decaying fruit from old relationships disappear. Infatuation is like the sun at noon—intense and short-lived. Relationships are sustained when individuals master their own emotional garden, which requires constant weeding, fertilizing, water, and ample sunlight.

The south wind moves through your territory of emotions. Just like the wizards in the Hopi legend, you can learn to face your fears and soothe your emotional pains. By casting one snowball at a time into any warm southern wind, you will eventually become master of your own destiny. The warmth and brilliance of the summer sun can defeat even the bitterest cold. Love can prevail in your life no matter what spiritual challenges come your way.

Although the south wind is filled with good intentions and passion, it also carries negative traits such as anger and fear. As you hone your navigational skills, when the south wind stirs, you will no longer be hindered by a self-defeating flapping sail, and will be able to steer your boat. If you desire to have a deeper, more meaningful relationship with your spirit, you must be prepared to constantly adjust your sails as you journey through life. Each cycle of your life will reveal new allies and teachers who can help.

South winds can be unpredictable, making it difficult to navigate. In many traditions they are viewed as adolescent winds. They also represent the winds that stir under a hot midday sun during the longest day of the year, and are conveyors of emotional storms. Remember, however, that summer rains can quickly refresh an overheated landscape. The southern winds are the most powerful yet subtle energies of your inner landscape. Without proper alignment of your inner compass, your emotions can cause you to lose your bearings. Taking personal responsibility for healing past trauma and upsets is crucial if you truly want to find peace. During your life you may experience illness, abuse, heartbreak, loss, or pain. Although challenges are inevitable, the manner in which you deal with them is always in your hands; emotional suffering is optional.

If you are diagnosed with an illness, you may find the solution when the southern winds are blowing. Western medicine merely treats the symptoms of disease, whereas shamans treat diseases as a whole. Removing symptoms may be the first step; then you need to align your mental, emotional, and spiritual components. Shamans believe diseases can be prevented before they manifest in the physical body. Some people are also able to heal chronic illnesses by restoring balance within. If dying from an illness turns out to be your spiritual destiny, the work you do in the south will help you to achieve peace as you sail your inner seas during your final days on earth.

In life, we are often attracted to, and fall in love with, people who possess traits that we lack. The bitter experience of finding out that the "other" person, place, or thing cannot complete us is one of the greatest lessons we can learn in the southern quadrant. As Karol Truman pointed out in her 1991 book of the same name, "Feelings buried alive never die."

THE EMOTIONS

Desires and needs reside in the south. In and of themselves, these are neither good nor bad, but if left unchecked, they can cast your ship onto perilous reefs. Anger, despair, loneliness, confusion, and frustration are signs that you have been blown off course. Some flaws in life can be removed, while others remain as vital points on your compass, enabling you to calculate your current position and make adjustments before moving on.

Learning to recognize the signposts of the south wind will help you to identify your feelings and recognize where they reside in your body. With this knowledge, you will become an inspired and skilled navigator of your inner world and be able to achieve and celebrate your dreams. As you orient to life using your body as a guide, you will become more receptive to the signals generated by your internal navigational system. Imagine your emotions as the needle of a compass providing all the information needed to chart a course of equanimity and purpose. As you awaken and become the observer of your emotions via physical sensations, you will learn to navigate safely through life no matter which way the wind(s) may be blowing.

Emotions are the magnetic variation on your personal compass that will keep you on course. Whenever you feel angry, look for resentment. Whenever you feel sad, look for the hurt. When you feel fear, where might you have lost faith? When you feel surprise, look for the mystery. When you feel joy, look for the presence. When you feel love, look for its source. Take note of where you feel these emotions; do they have a specific color or density? Are they lodged in a specific area of your body, or do they migrate to various locations?

Note: Reconnecting to your body does not guarantee perfect health. However, learning to observe the subtle changes in your body can help you achieve a state of inner peace. As you learn to navigate your emotional winds, physical detours like sickness or injury become blessings that can help you heal and grow. Used regularly, the awakening compass becomes a reliable tool to help you master your life, with the chief orienting point of your compass being *serenity.*

UNDERSTANDING YOUR FEELINGS

A fundamental understanding of your emotions is necessary for inner growth. Most people, however, do not know how they truly feel, which limits their ability to experience a fulfilling life. Six commonly accepted core emotions are happiness, sadness, anger, disgust, shock, and fear. Left unchecked, emotions can trigger an imbalance in the internal organs leading to illness, and paving the road for accidents and/or mental instability.

Feelings are expressions of emotional states that manifest as physical sensations in the body. If your pet dies, every corner of your house becomes an emotional trigger. Not only will you feel sad, but you may also have involuntary responses, which in turn send energy signals throughout your body. After the loss of my beloved pet, fearing that I might accidentally step on her tail made me wary and jumpy.

Because you are constantly being bombarded by sensory stimuli, it is easy to overlook or ignore a subtle ache. Emotional regressions are involuntary responses and overreactions when lingering impressions, memories, words, and actions go unattended in the physical body. It is an act of courageous healing to attend your feelings. Generally, a fight with a loved one that triggers hurt-filled words comes from repressed states of emotions. Impassioned situations like separation, divorce, and death can trigger the release of pent-up feelings, leading to anger disorders and other destructive winds. When anger fuels a raging storm, the people you love and whose actions you trust can change. Unhealed, anger can become peace-eradicating winds of destruction.

Like a tornado whipping through the landscape of our serenity, unresolved feelings such as anxiety, anger, sadness, and fear,
can take their toll and leave you stranded. According to the *Suwen*
(The Book of Plain Questions), unchecked emotions are the major
cause of illness.[3] The best way to feel more centered is by recali-
brating your inner emotional compass, which can reveal reasons
for the source of your distress.

Grounding on a regular basis is paramount to staying healthy,
for as we focus our attention on our body and natural surroundings, we begin to feel the rhythm of nature move through us
with a more consistent flow. Then, when a gusty wind hits our
sails (energetically speaking), we will not topple into the cold sea.
Often, grounding happens when you notice an eagle flying overhead, watch a deer as it eats an apple from a tree, or listen to a set
of jingling wind chimes. Take a daily walk in nature and remember that you are intrinsically connected to the world around you.

WHEN THE SOUTH WIND BLOWS

If your thoughts churn in your head like rolling clouds during
a summer thunderstorm, you may appreciate the origins of the
word *resentment*, which comes from the Latin root word meaning
"to refeel." Years ago, my psychiatrist explained to me that my
wind bursts of anger were my way of expressing pain. A sudden
downpour of feelings, including fear, confusion, embarrassment,
irritability, dismay, boredom, exhaustion, grief, insecurity, hope-
lessness, helplessness, jealousy, hate, and depression are good indicators that your needle is pointing south.

The stirring of southern winds signals the advent of something new. Every new beginning requires an emotional checkup.
Consider the phrase, "You must have gotten up on the wrong side
of the bed." Each morning you are provided with a new opportunity to see the world with fresh eyes. Heading into a south wind
requires you to constantly readjust your sails throughout the day.

CHAPTER 7

THE CARDINAL WIND
OF THE WEST (THE BODY)

O wild West Wind, thou breath of Autumn's being
Thou from whose unseen presence the leaves dead
Are driven like ghosts from an enchanter fleeing.[1]

— PERCY BYSSHE SHELLEY

An Iroquois legend states that after fire was born, air was created. Then Goah, the master of all wind gods, planted an animal
in each quadrant of the sky to watch each cardinal direction. He
placed a bear in the north, a moose in the east, a fawn in the
south, and in the west, he planted a mighty panther, a tempest
wind named Dajoji. As the keeper of the setting sun, and west
wind, Dajoji signaled the end of each daily cycle. To northern
Native Americans, the panther plays a significant role in witch-
craft, hunting, medicine, and healing. For southern Native Americans, panther sightings are associated with wealth, the earth, and
good fortune.

The west signifies harvest celebrations, the end of cycles,
destruction, and the physical body. In Percy Bysshe Shelley's
famous poem "Ode to the West Wind" (above), he describes
the cyclical process of death and decay required for birth and

regeneration: "Drive my dead thoughts over the universe, Like wither'd leaves, to quicken a new birth."[2]

The west marks the end of summer and the beginning of autumn. This time of the year is the perfect time to dance, celebrate, and retreat from the monotony of daily routines. Wind energies blowing in from the western quadrant can help you reap the rewards of your physical efforts. Just as the final months of a calendar year mark holidays that symbolize joy and celebration, we should enjoy the physical bounty of our labors as we reflect on the accomplishments of the previous seasons.

The west also represents the harvest, which denotes both the preservation and destruction of life—just like autumn, the season when crops are harvested and the fields are empty, but people's bellies are full and the sharpness of the cooler air stimulates the senses. The invigorating chill and colorful palette of autumn can easily grab our attention, putting us at ease and possibly making us complacent, but this is actually a time to be alert, with our senses fully awakened.

Many traditions view a pernicious west wind as a harbinger of death. In the Bible, the west wind warns of the end of time that will eventually bring forth the restoration and renewal of faith. Shamans view death as more than a once-in-a-lifetime experience. Death wears many disguises, among them the loss of innocence, physical death, or spiritual initiation. Like the natural cycles of night and day, we are continually dying and being reborn. When sunlight retreats into darkness, it is a blessing, allowing for the rejuvenation of our body, mind, and spirit.

A western wind possesses devious qualities, many of which are well hidden. Stepping over the finish line as you complete a project, relationship, or cherished goal can feel like crossing a suspension bridge in a harsh wind. You must stay focused and centered on each step to reach the other side of the gorge.

The light of the fire will keep the harsh winds at bay. This is not yet the time for rest or sleep. It is imperative that you are wide awake and in tune with your body.

THE BODY

You must be aware of your body if you want to navigate your personal map and explore the four territories. A west wind will direct your attention to the physical. Unlike the mind, the body is a visible form and loves to move. Caring for your physical self is an important aspect of waking up. Eating, walking, stretching, sex, exercise, and dancing are activities that can help you become aligned as you move through the cycles of your life. Because of our ability to reason in the east, and feel in the south, we are capable of fine-tuning our internal compass to make more informed choices about our physical health in the west. These choices allow the west to be a celebration of health and well-being. It is true that bodies are resilient and capable of self-renewing. Nonetheless, we should respect our bodies, like a boat captain who continually waxes the deck, replaces ropes, lubricates the pulleys, and repairs the sails.

Prior to your physical death, you may experience a series of debilitating symptoms as your body gradually withers away. Eventually, your mind consents, and your body collapses and finally expires. Exhaling your final breath (the wind of the body) brings you to a state of relief and peace.

To shamans, "dying" while living is a true initiation, a transformative process, usually brought about by unforeseen events, such as when a house burns down, a parent dies, or a company goes bankrupt. The "death" (or passing) of one thing always heralds the birth of another. When you get married, your life as a single person ends. Each choice you make will reflect how you move forward on the earth. The options you leave behind become dust in the wind. When you relocate to a new home, the life you lived in your old neighborhood withers away. When you graduate from school, the child you once were no longer exists. All "deaths" inevitably lead to "rebirths" and give us a chance to redefine ourselves. The appearance of wind gods and goddesses of the west indicate that we are leaving something behind and creating a void that can be filled with something new. It is an invitation to celebrate what has been, and who we are right now.

Christians believe in life after death, recognizing that death is merely a transition into a new life: a spiritual rebirth. In Hinduism, life and death combine in a repeating cycle known as reincarnation. Both traditions recognize that birth and death are not permanent. Indigenous medicine people know that we die many times before taking our final curtain call on the grand stage we call life.

RELATIONSHIPS

Falling in love is a physical magnetic event; attraction to another can happen in an instant. The hormones released when we fall in love trigger a kind of euphoria that may cause us to lose our bearings; Plato called this the "madness of the gods." When you are facing a west wind, your love will be tested. The west relates to issues such as disappointment and rejection, the logistics of cohabitation and income generation, the healthy expression of our sexuality, and all aspects of a sustainable partnership. As we awaken, our goal is to find the "right relationship," one that holds equality and propels us further forward on our journey toward wholeness, from which perspective we can become compassionate lovers.

ILLNESS AND HEALING

Unable to deal with the pressures of modern-day living, many people turn to medication for relief from both physical and mental/emotional ailments. According to the United States Center for Disease Control, antidepressants were the third most common prescription in 2008, and more than one out of every ten people over the age of 12 are prescribed these medications. However, those who do inner work typically rely less upon on prescribed medications than others. Their awakening compasses are better calibrated, which allows them to respond more effectively when symptoms of "the dark night of the soul" arise.

At some point in your life cycle, you will face the setting sun in the west: you will deal with your own aging process, as well as the aging of your friends and parents. As you age, you develop a better understanding of your body and its needs. As your parents age, you face your own mortality, offering you a chance to resolve unfinished business.

After the loss of her father, the elderly mother of one of my clients became demanding and required a great deal of attention. According to my client's worldview, this extended stay in her mother's western quadrant kept her from pursuing her own chosen activities. In order for her to move forward in her career, it was essential that she learn the spiritual art of navigating strong headwinds. During the course of navigating a relationship with another person, if you are stuck headlong into a wind, this could provide you with an opportunity to face the aging process from your own perspective.

WHEN THE WEST WIND BLOWS

The west wind is to the body as the south wind is to the emotions. Physical indicators of quality of health include a heightened sense of smell, acid indigestion, colds, flu, and other lung-related issues. These internal winds mirror the winds of the outer world. It is therefore interesting that the lungs are sensitive to the pernicious external winds responsible for conveying airborne illnesses into our bodies.

Winds blowing from the western quadrant of your life's map often serve as catalysts for the spiritual transition that the sixteenth-century mystic Saint John of the Cross termed *the dark night of the soul*. Busy lives do not allow for these types of experiences, wherein our sense of identity and stability is questioned. Keep in mind that dark nights of the soul often occur in midlife.

CHAPTER 8

THE CARDINAL WIND
OF THE NORTH (THE SPIRIT)

The wind blows to the south
and turns to the north;
round and round it goes,
ever returning on its course.

—ECCLESIASTES 1:6-7
NEW INTERNATIONAL VERSION (NIV)

Perhaps because their winter climate is so harsh and the corre-
sponding chilly nights so long, the legends of many far-northern
cultures speak of a hero who must defeat a monster in order to
rescue a captive spring and return it to its rightful place among
the people. In the Scandinavian folktale "Saving Spring," Old
Man Winter captures and imprisons spring. Oscar, a witty young
man, volunteers to make a treacherous trek to rescue it, despite
a warning that all his predecessors were transformed into wild
animals. Oscar is lulled into a deep sleep by the bitter cold of the
north. Upon waking, he realizes he has been shape-shifted into a
tiger. Driven by ravenous hunger, he forgets his original mission
and pursues a rabbit, and during a moment of clarity, Oscar wakes
from the spell, remembers his mission, and recognizes the rabbit
as his ally.

North winds stir your imagination, a place where the pursuit of spiritual excellence occurs. The catch is that the realization of our life's true purpose also means facing the shadowy sides of our personalities. In order for Oscar to serve his community effectively, he had to undergo a spiritual transformation and embrace his dualistic nature, which included a fierceness that originally made him uncomfortable.

You must consciously engage with the wind energies of the barren north again and again until you fully realize your human potential, which is to be of maximum service to others. Failure to tend to the task of your mind, emotions, and body can lead to neglect of your humanity. Symptoms include supporting profit over people, war over peace, and progress at the expense of the environment. The winds that blow from the northern quadrant of your life help you find acceptance of your shadow self. Only when Oscar overcame his fear of starvation was he able to return the vitality of spring to his village.

Chasing after the north wind is a reminder of our frivolous human experiences. Most people chase one illusionary goal after another, and never achieve happiness. Reconciling with the cold north wind teaches you that the wind cannot be caught and contained. The goal is an invisible wind of peaceful service.

THE NORTHERN LANDSCAPE

The north is a place of service. Your experiences in this quadrant will either be pleasant or arduous, depending on your choices and the attitude you bring to each challenge. Remember, large challenges present greater opportunities for spiritual growth.

Braving the north can be like walking a reluctant dog in snow, demanding your complete attention with every tug. Its sharp, cold grasp requires you to wear a warm overcoat. A question you must answer if you find yourself in the northern quadrant is, "Are friends only those who help us?" Many life lessons are gleaned from adversaries, so it is wise to consider the challenging energies of the wind gods and goddesses as opportunities to reconsider how you respond to threats. The north wind bore through the 2016 presidential election in America, creating a deep chasm within families, friends, and community. These adversarial bone-chilling winds of change stirred people into action to protect their perceived spiritual well-being. "For what shall it profit a man, if he shall gain the whole world, and lose his own soul?" (Mark 8:36)[1]

THE SPIRIT

Wisdom keepers have always known that everything is composed of energy, and all forms of life are spiritual in nature. When the Spanish conquistadors arrived in South America, the natives were polytheistic and openly embraced the idea of "more god," without realizing that their acquiescence to the European soldiers would soon force them to conceal their traditions and rituals. They were unaware that these missionaries were not adding to their abundant cosmology with hundreds of deities, but were instead promoting a single supreme God. If you remember to pursue your spiritual mission, even in secret, you won't have to worry about being transformed into a hungry tiger.

If you ever lose your spiritual bearings, it is wise to pause and reflect on the energies of the wind gods and goddesses currently frolicking in the north wind. Listen carefully to your inner compass, as your intuition uses it to whisper words of long-forgotten wisdom. Every time you engage these processes is a perfect occasion to make a sacred journey, a time for a contemplative retreat into nature. Relax, smile, and surrender to the peace and serenity in the stillness of your frozen northern caves.

While the energy of the north wind may appear passive on the surface, it is active below. The north is an essential gateway to a deeper spiritual realm residing within you, wherein lie powerful fertile energies. Like a Douglas fir rooted on the edge of a cliff, we stand poised and ready, waiting patiently for the winds of change to buffet and strengthen us.

Moments of wisdom and clarity can arise during yoga class, while hiking, in meditation, or when confronted by an unexpected gust of wind. There are many predictable patterns in our lives—the cycles of work and relationships, annual cycles, and astrological cycles, to name a few—but the darkness of night and unexpected problems can arise at any time, creating stress and discomfort in our lives. A northern wind chill signifies the end of such cycles.

Remember that self-realization is about developing clarity, focus, and discovery. Thus, your visit to the land of the north need not be a mission of darkness, sorrow, and suffering. It can be a time to pause and reflect before starting something new, to take a silent retreat or even an afternoon nap.

WHEN THE NORTH WIND BLOWS

Courage, strength, and patience are required when facing a north wind. We must be brave like the migrating reindeer as we enter uncharted territories. Our vision must be as clear as the Great Plains after a snowstorm. Friends, enemies, lovers, and teachers may come and go, but ultimately we have to plan our journey, draw our maps, and travel our spiritual paths alone. North winds demand that we make time and allow space for introspection.

Stand firm as you confront your enemies or pursue a deeper calling in your life. Be vigilant, for the monsters within will rear their ugly heads many times in your life. It is better to face your demons consciously when they reveal themselves, than to be ambushed by the ones you denied, which may lead to illness, loss, or tragedy.

In the Andes Mountains, young men of the Q'ero undergo initiation either by spending a night alone on a cold glacier, where they pray for a vision, or by jumping into an icy lagoon tethered to the shore by a rope. Such initiation rituals signify the commencement of a period of spiritual maturity wherein these men no longer require a teacher, and instead dedicate themselves to becoming one with nature. They ask the wind to bless their naked hearts with a new map for the future. Symbolic objects representing this spiritual experience are added to the medicine bundles they always carry with them. Like the Q'ero, we too gain valuable skills through our ice-cold initiations. When the cardinal winds blow in from the north, its messages pertain to the spiritual "medicine" we gain from meeting our challenges.

With spiritual awakening, there is an initial recognition and acceptance of a power greater than you. After surrendering to this power, you learn how to live in harmony with nature by making inner adjustments. Whenever a sustained chill fills the air, it may be the north wind reminding you to reset your sails.

At times, life can feel like we are walking through a harsh winter storm without a scarf, causing us to react to the winds with bitterness and rage. During these chilling experiences, we learn to exercise patience and practice tolerating the wind. As a wise teacher, the north sometimes employs tough love in order to align us with our destiny, or magnetic north. Spiritual advisors are great allies when you feel lost in a blizzard, so it is wise to cultivate these relationships throughout your travels. The north is a place where good habits make barren times easier to navigate.

In Feng Shui, a shamanic tradition from China, the north is said to govern the eternal natural recycling of water, from its evaporation from lakes and oceans into the heavens, eventually returning in the form of clouds and as replenishing rain. We all possess the water of wisdom. We are destined to sail through the territories of the north many times until the earth finally reabsorbs our bodies, and our moisture rises to the heavens for the last time.

MOVING INTO ACTION

These myths demonstrate that our ancestors throughout history celebrated and honored the four cardinal winds as spirit. From the longhouse of the plains' Indians tribes whose naming ceremonies included sending small children into the "midst of the wind," to the allegorical Scottish tale by George MacDonald, *At the Back of the North Wind*, which explains the mystery of death to a child, the winds of spirit have cooperated and shaped our human experience.

In Part III, you will learn some ancient but simple strategies to help you navigate life. The winds of spirit have existed since the beginning of time, and are available 24/7 to guide and assist you.

Part III

WHEN THE WIND BLOWS— NAVIGATING LIFE

CHAPTER 9

WIND MAGIC
THROUGHOUT HISTORY

"The weatherworker's and seamaster's calling upon wind and water were crafts already known by his pupils, but it was he who showed them why the true wizard uses such spells only at need, since to summon up such earthly forces is to change the earth of which they are a part."[1]

— URSULA K. LE GUIN

History shows that wind practices were used by hunter-gatherers, farmers, and sailors thousands of years ago. In Greenland, it was believed women who had given birth possessed the power to raise a storm using their blood-soaked sheets.[2] To lay a storm, the women would step outside, and fill their lungs with air, and exhale after returning inside.[3] You can use these sacred practices to influence your responses and navigate change in your life. Once you learn to cooperate, harness, and consciously harmonize your energy with the emanating forces of wind, you will be the master of your thoughts, emotions, body, and spirit.

Wind bath, wind knots, wind prayers, whistling up a wind, cutting the wind, bull roaring, and preparing wind flags are all techniques you can employ to navigate shifting winds. With a simple change in perspective, air magic can energize you, shift your direction, and expand your perception. Projects can gain momentum through your cooperation with the winds. A cool breeze can soften anger, and confusion dissipates when you listen to the wisdom of the wind. The arrival of Zephyrus brings new friends. Flurries of new opportunity magically appear. Once you acknowledge the powerful forces of nature, you will be able to rely on wind as a constant ally.

By harmonizing with the elements, you will become like a tree on the bluff that gently bends in acquiescence to the winds of change that take aim at your life. From the absolute calm of no wind, to the extreme force of hurricanes and tornados, you will learn that in every experience there are valuable lessons to be learned. You will feel protected.

WHISTLING UP A WIND

When I was a child, I was part of the Girl Scouts. One summer, we gathered in the Berkshire Hills each night before dinner on a pine-scented log porch to lift our voices to the wind. Songs like "They Call the Wind Maria" sailed into the forest.

Decades later, folk songs about nature still transport me back to those whimsical summer nights. Song lyrics hold mystical power; they are records of ancient history and mythology. You too can use your voice to call upon the wind, using time-tested lyrics or by creating your own. Using your voice to move energy can be done anytime, anywhere. Breath is a unified wind, a gateway to time and space that empowers you to speak and sing.

Another way of calling to the winds is with a whistle. Unlike most singing voices, whistles can hold a pure tone for longer time periods. The ancient ones knew about the power of whistling vessels. Pierced antler whistles dating to the Upper Paleolithic age (9000 BCE) have been found in Central and Western Europe.[4] Archaeologists conjecture that these tools were used for warning, hunting, healing rituals, and magic. Whistling vessels made of bone, hollowed reed, and wood are found worldwide. In Peru, there is a set of ancient pottery wind vessels still used for healing and ceremony. In Mexico, they used a high-pitched death whistle for transition rituals. In Appalachia, indigenous tribes carved wind whistles from alder. Tales of the Feadan, Irish tin whistle, go back to the third century BCE. In the tribal tale of Ailen, Tuatha Dé Danann, the chief of the faeries, would cast a sleeping spell over the inhabitants of the king's palace at Tara, in order to carry out mischievous deeds.[5] Sailing history has many tales of skilled whistlers who could charm the wind.

The jaguar-faced whistle used in wind work was discovered by chance one day at a pyramid site in Mexico. There was a vendor selling a replica of the ancient death whistle, constructed from clay and resin. Still clueless as to where the winds were taking me, I purchased a few as souvenirs and took up the art of wind whistling for healing and magic. One night as I was calling in the winds during a ceremony, the participants marveled as the forces of nature arrived on command, blowing open a door in one direction, while moving water across the pool in another direction. I then used my whistle to conjure up a steady wind at the fire.

Blowing into the wind whistle changes your perception by altering brain waves. Whistles provide expedient access into other states of consciousness. Whistles create a beat frequency that elevates consciousness, lowers your heartbeat, and enhances your body's natural healing potential.[6] When I feel out of sorts, blowing into a whistle changes my perspective. Clients immediately feel the shift in energy once I begin to blow the jaguar whistle.

When used to summon the inner winds, the tones and qualities of the airflow change depending upon the inner wind being called forth. One time, with a hearty blow, I whistled in the wind goddess Oyá for a client to hasten her cab ride across Manhattan, while another time she strategically called upon Vayu while writing her historical novel. One day while teaching a webinar, the Teutonic wind goddess Holle (Hulda) barged in with supreme sway, slamming the front door shut as she entered. She arrived and created order on the call. One listener described this moment when a chill wind entered her open window, toppling a stack of unfiled papers. Over time, I learned that working in harmony with these wind energies helped clients navigate through most of life's challenges. You too can summon a wind by randomly opening a page in Part IV and then inviting the wind by calling to it three times, by singing or whistling.

Remember that no matter how good a magician you are, the winds have their own divine nature and will. Tornados may breach your life-scape, or a good-spirited Ventoline (Spanish wind fairy) may slap you with a soft wake-up breeze. Nature is always available to guide you if you are paying attention.

CEASING THE WINDS

Storms will rage in your life in the form of arguments, sleepless nights, loss, moving, and severe weather conditions. Call upon a wind to find shelter from its effects. One wind believer learned that a storm was brewing that could bring 15 inches of rain, causing mass flooding. She called upon Yaponcha, the Hopi wind of moderation, to assist as she prepared her family for the storm. According to ancient mythology, the Hopi clan had survived the Great Flood and emerged to create a new civilization. This wind believer reported back the following day that they only received 2.3 inches in her town.

When stirring winds disrupt your sleep, you can ask them to quiet. Ask your swirling mind to become still: "Taba, it is enough, please give me rest." The winds will honor your request, if you ask with sincerity and have faith in their power. However, with some winds, you will need to be stern: "TABA. It is ENOUGH."

One method you could try is to go out into a storm with a knife in hand (not when there is lightning, please!) and face the wind. Hold the knife out in front of you and slice the wind, beginning with your hand extended above your head, and moving down toward the earth.

Another method used by the ancient ones was to spit into the direction of the wind three times, and then go indoors and wait patiently for the storm to pass. Over the years, spitting into the wind has become synonymous with time-wasting pursuits. While our wind-believing hats are off to those naysayers, you may want to ceremoniously stand at a right angle to the wind when you spit, or if spitting directly into the wind, duck.

BULLROARING

Bullroarers are long, flat engraved wooden blades, pierced with a hole attached to a string. For the Aboriginal tribes of Australia, the bullroarer is perceived as the voice of God, and used for communicating over long distances, and during ceremony. The Southwest Plains Indians used bullroarers for male initiation ceremonies, in rituals for rain, and to bring a warm wind to melt snow.[7] The medicine man cuts through the air, spinning the wood lasso-style. This creates a gap in the timeline for the healing spirits to enter or for noncompliant spirits to exit. The high-pitched sound has been considered the voice of Spirit, the sound of rain, and was used to call the village and silence people during ceremony.

The art of commanding air using this tool will take some practice. You will want to open sacred space (you can use the wind invocation in Chapter 11). Stand on a mound with plenty of airspace and twirl the bullroarer above your head. You will hear a high-pitched humming noise. Then place your intention on calling forth a wind of spirit for guidance, clarity, or a sign. Be careful when using a bullroarer, because you are holding a blade and creating a tremendous force with every spin. This is not something to use amidst a crowd or in the heart of a city.

Weather workers also use Scotch broom in a similar fashion to clear the air before rituals and ceremonies. Sweeping before ceremony serves the purpose of setting the space, and removing stagnant energy. Notice the movement of air the next time you sweep your home. Sweep with the intention of clearing out all negative, unwanted, and uninvited energies and thoughts as you sweep. Give them to the wind. These practices are good for creating sacred space at a fire or while clearing land.

81

WIND FLAGS

Add some colorful wind flags to your home to brighten up your spirit, observe changes in intensity and direction of the wind, spread peace, and to catch *chi* (energy). Peace flags predate Buddhism in Tibet, fluttering in the wind over mountain passes and rivers in Tibet for over 2,000 years, beginning with the Bon shamans.[8] Many cultures use colored flags to represent the five elements. Wind flags are symbols of victory, health, and peace. The Lakota tie prayer flags during their Inipi ceremonies, sun dances, and vision quests. The use of flags to carry messages to distant gods is almost as old as the wind.

While the wind communicates without words, sutras or prayers are often inscribed on flags. Symbols are useful reminders and stimulate the subconscious. One popular Tibetan flag symbol is the Wind Horse (*Lungta*), who rides the wind and brings stability, good fortune, and is powerfully present.[9] Prayer symbols are often grouped together; the eight auspicious Tashi Targye (Tibetan flags) include happiness, fulfillment, purity, enlightenment teachings, meditation, wisdom, universal law, and protection from negative energy.[10]

In your wind practices, you can assemble prayer ties and flags for every ceremony. One practice you can try is to exchange blessings with the creator by assembling prayer flags to hang vertically on a string. As you decorate your flag, be mindful and contemplate the wisdom of each cardinal direction. Begin your flags in the east, the home of the rising sun.

You may follow the directions below or work with your own inner harmony; the important factors are prayer and intention.

Supplies:
Five 8 x 8-inch squares of colored fabric: red, white, green, blue, and yellow
Fabric paint markers
Enough string to connect the five squares
Scissors or a hole punch

Step One: Using your creativity and imagination, paint each flag with the fabric marker.

A great way to establish a spiritual connection is to tie flags of various colors onto a string. Each color represents one of the five elements: blue for wind or ether, white for air, red for fire, green for water, and yellow for earth.[11]

Begin with the red flag, which symbolizes the wisdom of the mind in the east. As you awaken, your vision becomes a clear vessel of service.

Next, decorate the harmonizing white flag of the south, the place of your emotions; visualize prayers of balanced needs and desires.

The green flag of the west will represent the physical act of kindness that you adhere to in your life.

The blue flag of compassion will go next. This flag is a symbol of the cardinal north wind, the place of spirit on your awakening compass.

The final flag on your string is the yellow flag, found in the central pin of your body's awakening compass, which symbolizes the perfect wisdom achieved upon a radical awakening.

Step Two: On each flag, punch a hole one inch from each of the top corners. String the red, white, green, blue, and yellow flags through the holes, from left to right.

Step Three: Once you have assembled your flags, find a suitable spot in your environment to hang them. You can craft a pole, or hang the flags from a tree. Let the wind guide you.

In all ceremonies, it is wise to say a prayer of gratitude before you begin and upon completion of your work. Invite friends to witness your ceremony. Then let the winds dance your prayers up to the heavens.

The practices in this chapter will make it evident that our ancestors understood the magnificent power of air that made magic available to humans. Your connection to nature will expand as you place your awareness on the air that moves through your life.

As you awaken, you become increasingly in awe of nature, in all its chaotic glory. While many external aspects of nature are beyond your immediate grasp, learning to see your complimentary participation will aid your awakening. At first glance you may begin to witness subtle movement of air, or even winds barreling through your life, and you may feel lost without a map. The next chapters offer hope. The basic practices of wind work of prayer, meditation, and wind breath can calm the storm. Roots run deep when you find your center, and being grounded in your body is an essential first step.

CHAPTER 10

FINDING YOUR CENTER

PRAYER AND MEDITATION

During my early years as a recovering alcoholic, I was blessed with the gift of prayer. At first I felt like a beggar, until an astute guide from Alcoholics Anonymous explained that prayer is simply a method for organizing requests to spirit. Meditation is the practice of patiently waiting for the answer. Back then, my list of unfulfilled needs and desires was long. Years later in Southern California, as I sat on the hard-packed desert sand in the Inipi (sweat lodge), I felt embarrassed by my inability to vocalize my heartfelt prayers. While other participants spoke eloquently, my demands felt like egocentric complaints about how I had been wronged and forsaken. Decades later, during my awakening, I experienced a radical shift in awareness. My list of demands grew shorter and shorter, and my requests to Spirit became appeals on behalf of others. I thanked the winds of spirit for my first breath, and the air that connected me to them. I realized that I have everything I need. As I grew fluent in prayer, I became an active participant in creating my own satisfaction and eventually learned to cooperate with the forces of nature residing within me.

Prayer and meditation tame your inner winds. Taking simple steps such as sitting before your altar or taking a wind walk in nature will allow peace to enter your heart. While disease, divorce, work, and family dynamics can be tumultuous storms, the gentle flickering flame of a candle burning on a table can provide a comforting wind of peace, and illuminate the darkness when you are feeling lost. The invisible power of prayer is like the wind; its effects become apparent in retrospect.

Here are a few simple suggestions to get started.

- **Build an altar.** Pick a special place in your home where you can ask the winds of spirit to provide guidance. This can be a special chair in your home or a place in your garden. Adding a small table is a great idea. You can adorn this area with meaningful artifacts: statues of saints, a pouch of winds of spirit cards (used to evoke the divine wisdom of the companion wind spirits), tapestries, rocks, live flowers, a gratitude jar, or other containers. Ideally, the altar should face east, a region of light and new beginnings. Every day is an opportunity for new winds to grace your life. Power builds within as you return to your sacred space daily and add more prayers. Keep it simple. In this complex digital world, this is a place where the graceful winds can enter your heart.

- **Visit your sacred spot daily.** Replenish with fresh-cut flowers. Make offerings of fruit. Keep the area clean. Keep free of clutter. I keep a gratitude jar and add a thankful word daily.

- **Begin every day with a gratitude prayer.** Although saying "Thank you" is a good way to express your gratitude, you can also try other prayers such as the wind invocation found at in Chapter 11. The act of praying helps you move from the mundane to the mystical.

- **Organize your requests.** Be clear, concise, and positive. Express your appeal in the past tense, as if your answers have already been delivered on the breath of a wind. For example, if you are struggling with an illness, say, "Thank you, Spirit, for my perfect health."

- **Clear your consciousness.** Begin by sitting for a few minutes daily. As you cultivate your meditation practice, you will find your timing sweet spot. While some people sit daily for hours, others find that 10 minutes every morning fits their schedule. I prefer a daily walk. Thoughts will arise, disrupting your meditative flow. Do not resist; instead, offer them to the fluffy cumulus clouds, floating by in the wind. Early in my awakening, I was plagued with obsessive thinking. I developed an ongoing practice of putting debilitating ideas into imagined hot air balloons to drift away. Momentary emptiness allows your mind and heart to open up to guidance and clear direction.

WIND WALK

Sitting still in front of an altar day after day isn't an activity that appeals to everyone. Fortunately, for these good folks who prefer to straighten their thinking by being physically active, wind walking is a great way to go.[1] This practice works best when your solo intention is to be present with the wind while you walk. In the course of my life, I have met many people who find peace by hiking, gardening, and wind walking. Feeling confused at the age of 30, I was advised by my therapist to ask myself a single question, put it aside, and then take an evening walk. She claimed that I would feel better and receive guidance after a lengthy stroll. In fact, this book was inspired by, and many chapters were subsequently rewritten after, an evening's wind walk.

Wind walking keeps your body aligned to magnetic north and is a great way to find answers to life's pressing problems. I tend to take these grounding meditation walks by myself, later in the day, and they keep me present and centered. During this contemplative time, the winds of spirit know they will have my ear.

Here are a few suggestions to help you get started with this practice:

- **Find a time that works best for you.** Routines keep you on track. Good habits prepare you for whatever winds may be blowing. As a line cook, I was taught to perform simple repetitive tasks, so that when the restaurant was full, and tickets filled the window, my good habits would assure that every plate was consistent and I never drowned at sea during the storm.

- **Unplug.** As you cross over nature's threshold, go it alone. While you can carry your phone for comfort, or to catch an inspiring landscape, put it in airplane mode. Nature offers a symphony of healing music for those whose inner ears are open.

- **Ask a question.** Wind walks can provide intuitive guidance. Step out the door, ask one simple question. Here are some examples: *What is the prevailing wind in my life? Where should I focus my attention?* Open your heart, mind, and soul with the breeze before walking. This will ensure that you have Spirit's attention. You will actually feel the air nudging you to move forward. Notice the speed and intensity of the moving air.

- **Walk wherever you are.** If you live in a city, even a groomed, tree-lined park can reconnect you to nature. If you are in a big city, remember to be aware of the leaves moving in the trees, look up at the sky, and watch as the wind changes the color of the swaying grass. Is the breeze moving with or against you as you walk? Ideally, walk for at least 20 minutes.

- **Pay attention to every step.** Answers come in many ways. Focus on each physical step you take, feel the earth beneath your feet as you walk, inhale the scented air, touch a blade of grass, listen to the leaves rustling in the breeze, and bring your awareness into your mouth. Notice the changes in your surroundings over the course of a month. As you walk, witness the signs and synchronicities. While you will always feel better following a wind walk, the answer to your question may come as a surprise or from an unexpected source. Engaging in this practice on a regular basis will help you to become a competent sailor who follows the guidance of the winds of spirit.

- **Thank the wind.** Gratitude is the key to happiness. Gratitude aligns you to the perfection that already exists in your life. Wind is the essential element that sustains all life, so remember to say thank you. Every answer you will ever need awaits you in the winds of spirit.

WIND BREATH

Wind is breath that connects you to everything in the present moment. Inspiration is a dynamic link between your conscious, superconscious, and subconscious states of awareness. The air you inhale has been imbued with the consciousness of all living things since the beginning of time. As you exhale, you complete the breath cycle. One way to get balanced is to blow your wind whistle. The act of exhaling into the mouthpiece moves the air in your lungs, anchors your feet into the ground, and connects you firmly to the earth. The ancient ones knew the importance of wind whistling. If you do not have a whistle, you can still do the breathing exercise by placing your awareness on your breath, as the air rises and falls in your lungs.

Breathing connects you to wind. Every living being on the planet shares the same air. This seemingly small action of conscious breathing, or blowing your wind instrument is your passport to a sacred awakening that keeps you connected to nature. Answers to your most pressing concerns can be accessed through the breath of the present moment.

It is extremely important to respect and protect the air you breathe. Awakening and protecting the earth are one and the same. Graceful healing winds, or merciless storms of pollution can travel around the world in a few days. Clean air is crucial for good health and the well-being of Mother Earth and its inhabitants.

We take our ability to breathe, as well as wind, for granted. It is important to start every day with "Thank you." It remains a mystery just how the breath remembers to continue. Observe the manner in which you, and others, breathe.

Watch a cat, dog, or baby as it sleeps. Their breath is intuitive and rhythmic. Breath is the fuel that sustains energy. As you reconnect the wind to your abdomen, your mind expands, and blockages that prevent you from being present in the moment gradually dissipate. With persistent practice, you will undergo a metamorphosis and wake up *changed*.

As you learn to place your attention on your breath, you become the master of your inner winds. The energy in your body begins to respond like a finely tuned compass needle as you learn to consciously navigate the regions of your mind, emotions, body, and spirit. Whenever you feel tense, stop and focus on your breath.

CONNECTED BREATH PROCESS

Many of the processes in this section build upon this exercise of connected wind breathing. If you have a whistling vessel, please use it for this exercise to enhance your experience. One-of-a-kind wind whistles are available for purchase at ThePracticalShaman.com.

Step One: (Better results when practiced outdoors.) Stand with the wind at your back; facing the wind while breathing actually inhibits your breath. Balance your body by spreading your feet about shoulder width apart, and bend your knees slightly. Close your eyes. Visualize your diaphragm extending downward as you inhale the winds of love through your nose. Air moves naturally into the low-pressure zone, where more space is available. Shallow breathing goes against nature, which seeks to expand your oxygen intake.

Step Two: Close your eyes. As you inhale, you are catching—but not forcing—wind into your lungs. Place your hands on your abdomen. Feel it rise and fall as you inhale and exhale.

Draw this breath slowly into your abdomen (about four fingers below your navel, toward the back, near the base of your spine). Hold this life force energy as you slowly count to 10. As you gradually exhale (blow into the whistle), imagine the steady wind created by your breath moving into the earth, grounding you as you connect with the pull of magnetic north. Imagine your feet as tree roots reaching deep into the belly of Mother Earth and connecting you with the center of the planet's magnetic field. Allow the magnetic energy to rise up through the roots of your body and enter your spine, which is the center pin of the awakening compass in your physical body. Allow the energy to vibrate throughout your core. This energy will bring your body into complete alignment with the natural pulse of the earth.

Step Three: On your second breath, pull the air from the light of sun, visualizing this light filling up your lungs and your entire inner cavity. Hold this light as you slowly count to 10. As you gradually exhale (blow into the whistle), imagine the steady wind created by your breath rising into the atmosphere, connecting you to everything that moves and flows in the universe. Continue extending your breath outward as the energy in your core flows out to the heavens and stars. As you exhale, visualize your breath as a wind that releases negative emotions, blockages, and unwanted thoughts.

Some people experience physical sensations when they anchor; others see colors and/or hear sounds. Over time your perceptions will evolve. Trust that whatever you experience is real.

Step Four: As you inhale the third wind breath, bring it in from the universe, and watch how it flows in from the top of your head, down your spine, and circles back up. The air you inhale is the wind of love, which has traveled around the planet collecting the energy that you require to enliven your hopes and dreams. Watch as this Taurus of love energy builds in intensity. Allow the magnetic energy to rise and flow through the roots of your body and enter your spine, which is the central pin of your inner awakening compass. The awakening compass is your body, which acts a meter to let you know whether you are on or off course. With practice, you will know exactly when you are tuned in, or out of kilter.

Let the wind energy flow and vibrate your core. This energy will realign you with the present moment every time.

Imagine your breath expanding out into vast expanses of the universe. As you exhale, envision your breath as a sacred wind. Focus your attention on the space around you. Observe the places in your body where the air is constricted, preventing the wind from flowing outward. When I blow into my wind whistle, I immediately connect to a protective frequency of energy.

In that space, you can consciously let go.

Trust the authenticity of your experiences. When I breathe with my whistle, I move to an extraordinary place where time stands still. When I continue with the next step, everything becomes clear and takes care of itself.

Close your eyes and establish a pattern of steady, rhythmic breathing. Allow yourself to pull in the energy from the wind on your in-breath, and then release the same energy to the heavens on the out-breath. When you are calm, you are in your center point, a place where everything exists as a sacred potentiality.

Step Five: When you feel complete, slowly open your eyes. Move your body. Spend a minute contemplating what you have just experienced.

With practice, you will become increasingly aware of the power of nature. You will realize that your participation is complimentary, and cooperation with the winds of spirit is essential if you wish to achieve joy, peace, and prosperity as you navigate through life. Conscious breathing calms the inner winds.

The quest to find peace in your heart will grow stronger as you begin to utilize the powerful tools of wind work. Prayer and wind breath are joyful preparations for the meditative exercises in this book, including the weather vane process, wind bath, wind knots, commanding an inner wind, removing resistance to change, and preparing wind flags.

CHAPTER 11

CALIBRATING YOUR INNER
AWAKENING COMPASS

When you integrate wind wisdom into everything you do, navigating through the challenges of daily life becomes much easier. To begin your inner journey, it is helpful to know where you are at all times. The fundamental organizing principles discussed in Part II will show you how to adapt to change. I call these your inner awakening compass. Familiarizing yourself with the territories of the cardinal wind will help you determine your precise experiential location. Aligning your inner compass could be beneficial prior to making an important telephone call, going out on a date, beginning a new endeavor, feeling lost, or to find balance and equanimity before beginning your day. Your body is a dynamic system that contains all the guidance needed to navigate life, if only you are willing to listen to it. Before undertaking any endeavor, it is important to be aware if you are sourcing from your mind, emotions, physical body, or spirit. If your body is exhausted and you go to speak to your boss about a promotion and present reasons to support your case, you may lack the inner strength to effectively present your case. Awareness of your cycle allows you to respond and take action when the winds of grace opens a door. Keep in mind that your body is a dynamic compass, aligned to your personal magnetic north.

Magnetic north is your sweet spot. When you ride the winds of change with passion, your needs are met, you obtain measurable results, and life is a joyful experience of serving others each and every day.

The following five-step processes will help you determine your current coordinates, identify the prevailing cardinal wind, and properly calibrate your inner awakening compass.

Step One: Invoke the Cardinal Wind Gods

Start by calling up the cardinal winds, which are the gods that oversee the four quadrants (territories) of the map. Use the invocation below, or create your own once you become familiar with the energetic themes of each cardinal territory. The reason for calling upon these gods is to inform them and you that you are moving into a place outside of time and space known to shamans as nonordinary reality. This heightened state of clarity and balance allows you to safely navigate through life with joy and confidence.

WIND INVOCATION TO OPEN UP YOUR SACRED SPACE (SACRED CIRCLE)

When you call upon the cardinal wind gods and goddesses, you are indicating to the spirits that you are ready to participate in a contemplative ceremony. This invocation is an adaptation of the traditional ceremony of the Maori people of New Zealand (in their language, Aotearoa), which prepares male initiates for a spiritual experience (fishing trip) where they seek to win favor from the wind gods.

Make your reading a joyous occasion. Begin by laughing. "Ha-ha-ha." Then say:

> I am calling on the divine winds.
> Eurus of the east, Notus from the south, Zephyrus of the west, and Boreas in the north.
> Come here today to help me navigate my life.
> The wind feeds my life.

The wind renews.
The wind is prosperous.
There are many sacred gifts in the wind.
The wind reveals.
The wind expands.
The wind is generous.
The wind lives within me.
The wind offers a sweet melody.
I share my gifts to the world by offering them to the wind.
My body is borrowed from the earth while my spirit flies free like the wind.
I am grateful to the winds for this reading.
Blessed be.

The sensation of a breeze indicates the presence of spirit. Now you can begin.

Step Two: Anchor Yourself in Mother Earth

Stand with your feet spread apart, about shoulder width, with knees slightly bent. Close your eyes.

Step Three: Wind Breath

Find step-by-step instructions in Chapter 10. Close your eyes and establish a steady rhythm with your breath. Allow yourself to pull in the energy from the wind on your in-breath, and release the same energy to the heavens on the out-breath. When you are calm, you are in your center point, a place where everything exists as a sacred potentiality.

Step Four: Finding Your Cardinal Wind

In order to fully understand your current situation, you need to know which quadrant of the map the cardinal wind is coming from. These are the major themes that everyone experiences in life. Set your mind free to imagine yourself standing in your favorite spot in nature. With your eyes closed, observe your surroundings, inhale the aromas, feel the sensations, and listen carefully. Imagine there is a path before you, and as you walk up this path, take note of which direction you are heading—is it east, south, west, or north? You might actually see a signpost in your mind's eye; still other clues can be the position of the sun, the moon, a body of water, or a mountain. If you are uncertain, ask, "Which way am I heading?"

Once you start moving in a specific direction, open your eyes. Do not second-guess your choice. Trust your inner compass. There are no wrong answers, and all is well. This technique is useful for pinpointing the exact location of a single issue in your life. To learn more about the themes for this specific territory, revisit Part II.

Step Five: Closing Sacred Space

The process of invoking the winds should not be taken lightly. In an old maritime story about "purchasing" the wind, the captain of a boat stranded at sea is advised by the cook to stop cursing at the winds, and offer up thanks. The captain then tosses a fifty-cent piece into the sea. Within minutes, a gale-force wind appears and wreaks havoc on the ship. Working with the wind energies in your life is no different. Gratitude provides wind power.

Wind work is sacred, and therefore you should have an intimate, harmonious, and respectful relationship with the wind and nature. Despite the losses incurred, the captain was thrilled to discover that he was able call up the wind. Every experience counts when you add it to your wisdom chest. As the story goes, the captain realized that the next time he needed a wind to sail home, using a nickel would suffice. Like the captain, you will become increasingly aware of wind intensity, and how much is needed to get the job done.

When you first make changes in your life, you can experience an adverse reaction, like the gale-force winds that tore apart the captain's sails. For instance, if you gave up sugar, you might suddenly crave sweets, become constipated, develop a headache, or feel like taking daily naps. The more you do this work, the more aligned your inner awakening compass will be with your magnetic north, and the less agitated you are likely to feel after doing energy work.

No matter which cardinal wind god shows up in your meditation, be like the captain and remember to express your gratitude. Once your meditation is complete, close the sacred circle. Saying a simple thank-you will suffice, or you may recite the following prayer as an expression of gratitude.

Great wind which gathers strength,

Lasting wind,

A new day comes.

Great wind from above,

Lasting wind,

Close up this reading as the soft South Wind.

Great wind, lasting wind,

This reading is done.

Great wind, living wind,

Lasting wind,

Sacred is thy guidance.

Thank you, Eurus; return to the light.

Thank you, Notus; I welcome your light rains.

Thank you, Zephyrus; I am grateful
for your harvest winds.

Thank you, Boreas; please return to the cave
beyond the farthest mountain.

I dismiss the wind.

This practice is useful any time you feel lost. You may also choose to engage in a longer, more ceremonial process four times a year during the winter/summer solstices and spring/autumn equinoxes. This system works better when the body is receptive to ancient wind wisdom. As you continue to practice, you will witness how these winds of spirit can help you accomplish your goals, realize your dreams, and improve your relationships. You will be like a tree whose roots are firmly planted deep inside the nourishing soil as your branches and leaves undulate and quiver in the wind. From this vantage point, your body will become a finely tuned weather vane, aware of subtle, life-altering events.

CHAPTER 12

WEATHER VANE PROCESS: STAYING BALANCED DURING CHANGING WINDS

Weather vanes are man-made devices that indicate which direction the wind is blowing. It is their function, to turn with the wind, while remaining fixed in one place. This ancient system of wind tracking can be a very useful tool in your daily life. In "The Fable of the Willow," found on plate 44 of the fragmented ancient Babylonian tablets, dating from 1000–2000 BCE, there is a reference to sailors testing the wind by observing the bird of the wind perched on top of a temple in Nippur.[1] Sitting atop the original roof of the famed Greek Tower of Winds, there was a weather vane, a spinning bronze Triton holding a wand in his right hand.[2] This sacred temple was used for ceremonies, seasonal rituals, and community gatherings. The weather vane was vital, because the Greeks believed a slight change of breeze could indicate approaching storms, droughts, change of season, or time of day. Although elaborate satellite tracking systems have replaced ornate flags as predictors of changes in nature, weather vanes are still used throughout the world. As a creative expression of the human spirit, decorative whirligigs are both functional and architectural.

A weather vane is a finely balanced tool that consists of a central, fixed upright pivot, with a sail and a pointer at opposite ends. When the weight of the pointer and sail are evenly distributed, the weather vane points to and moves with the prevailing wind. When unbalanced, resistance is created at the pivot, and the weather vane is unable to spin freely and give a proper guidance. This same principle also applies to your body, mind, heart, and soul.

Learning to interpret your own weather vane signals will help you gravitate toward your awakening. This simple practice will help you to determine your current resistance point (pivot) and inner wind of guidance (sail) and point to the cardinal directional wind (pointer) where you are stuck. Removing obstacles and resistance is vital for balance and success. As the force of resistance is reduced, it becomes easier to move toward your magnetic north. Still, resistance is useful, as it highlights areas in your life where attention is required. This weather vane process can help you strike a balance between your current landscape (ego) and your magnetic north (god self). Finding a balance helps you identify and remove blockages, enabling you to move easily forward on your life path.

PIVOT: BALANCE POINT

In order for a weather vane to spin freely, the central pin must be free of resistance. As resistance is removed, your inner winds and cardinal winds achieve a state of equilibrium. A balanced distribution minimizes obstruction, allowing your weather vane to spin freely in shifting winds. It is important to remember that wind always blows in the present moment. If your goals and dreams are long-range weather forecasts, it is essential to bring your attention back to the here and now. Studying your current wind pattern will empower you to navigate safely through the trials and tribulations of daily life.

Step One: Identify disturbances in your body, emotions, mind, and soul. Friction can be caused by positive or negative thoughts, feelings, physical sensations, or spiritual imbalance. They can be as simple as not knowing how to organize your day, waking up tired, being disturbed by current events, anticipation, excitement, longing, and stress.

Step Two: Take three deep wind breaths. As you engage with the wind, inhale slowly while counting to 10. Hold your breath for 10 seconds, and slowly exhale as you count to 10 again. Repeat at least two more times. Complete instructions are in Chapter 10.

Step Three: Identify your current issue, question, or concern. Focus on a single event in your life. Consider your current situation and ask a question such as:

- "How can I best organize my workday?"
- "How can I stay calm today when I am surrounded by chaos?"
- "Where shall I find the answer that will allow me to move forward?"
- "Who can help me perform a task effortlessly?"
- "What steps can I take toward finding a suitable partner?"
- "How can I help my child excel on his/her exam?"

Certain projects such as writing a book, getting a degree, or becoming debt-free can take many years to complete. Every gust of wind can help you move forward. Sometimes, moving air could be the wind answering your questions and helping you to reframe your path. Other times, a gentle breeze might inspire you to take a contemplative stroll through the woods.

To achieve balance and harmony on your daily weather vane, you need to minimize the contrary wind of your current battle. Progress is effortless if you yield to the wisdom of spirit. Once you set a goal, offer it up to the wind. Then, every day afterward, do at least one thing to move your plan forward.

Step Four: Determine your current headwind. The headwind is the wind opposing your forward movement. Close your eyes. On the screen of your inner eye, imagine yourself standing in your favorite spot in nature. Observe your surroundings, inhale the aromas, feel the sensations, and listen carefully. A gentle wind blows toward you. The path is blocked before you. Observe any obstruction such as a tree, a closed gate, a boulder, etc. As you walk toward this barricade, take note of which direction you are heading—is it north, east, south, or west? Once you gain clarity about the direction of the roadblock, you can open your eyes. Do not second-guess your choice. Trust your inner compass. Alternatively, you can open any page randomly in Part III of this book to identify your current cardinal territory.

This cardinal wind will serve as the underlying theme for the interpretation of your weather vane. Keep in mind that east represents beliefs and new beginnings, south represents needs and desires, west represents physical endings and celebrations, and north represents spiritual pursuits and service. When faced with an exciting opportunity to launch a new project, a certain woman felt a pang in her solar plexis, which prevented her from taking the next indicated step forward. In her meditation, she found herself at the base of a snow-covered eastern mountain range, with a strong gale-force wind blowing in her face, causing her to freeze in her tracks. Upon examining her ideas, she realized that her thinking had been overambitious, keeping her stuck. This experience was a reminder to slow down and approach this new venture systematically, one step at a time.

Step Five: Open this book randomly to a wind in Part IV. Determine your current cardinal wind direction, and read the relevant description of the wind god or goddess you have turned to. This is the sail area of the weather vane, providing the wind of momentum and movement for your day. This movement is opposite to your arrow or direction of travel, the emanating energy that will keep you focused and get you moving forward. Throughout the day, call upon the wind god/goddess you have selected to assist you.

Example: You feel powerless and small in the face of current events happening elsewhere on the planet. You ask, "What can I do to help today?" You determine that your cardinal wind is blowing from the northern territory, preventing you from aligning with spirit. In Step Five, you turned to the Korean wind goddess Yeongdeung Halmang. Evoke this goddess of balance and she will rush toward you from the north and show you how to be of service to something greater than yourself by being in balance. Over the course of the day, you may be provided with opportunities to give of yourself. This may be as small as picking up trash, or it may be something greater, like donating to the Sierra Club. Each conscious action you take, be it large or small, will make a difference.

This process can be repeated often. The winds will become your trusted allies as you navigate through life.

Step Six: Close your sacred space. Once your meditation is completed, it is good practice to say a simple thank you; or you may recite the closing prayer from Chapter 11 as an expression of gratitude.

CHAPTER 13

WIND BATH

A wind bath is a great exercise for restoring internal harmony and balance. Simply stated, wind washing is using nature's supreme cleanser, the movement of air, to strip away all excess energy from your body's energetic field. One day, while standing on the edge of a bluff, a pine-scented wind blew straight through the core of my being, carrying away the deep exhaustion caused by a multiday drive. Now, whenever I feel stressed, I purposely call on the wind for relief.

Wind baths can relieve tension and stress by sweeping away your troubles. All you need is a steady current of air. To perform the following clearing exercise, wear loose clothing, as tight fabric can bind and catch the wind. If you have long hair, loosen it, and set your hair free. This exercise also works to clear stagnant energy from your home or property.

Step One: Identify an issue. Identify anything that is disrupting your peace of mind—physically, mentally, emotionally, or spiritually. Identify the issue by name, either out loud or silently. Example: "My shoulder hurts."

Pay close attention to your body as you state the issue. How does the declaration make you feel? For example, are you sad, tense, doubtful, or afraid? Locate the source of this emotion in your body. Breathe in again while focusing on your object (e.g., your hurting knee) and mentally record the sensations you experience.

Investigate the significance of your issue. For instance, the pain in your knee could be related to responsibility. Shoulders are designed to support the weight of your head, and are instrumental when carrying supplies. Ask yourself, "Where am I shouldering a burden or something heavy?" As you look within, identify any heaviness inside your body. Trust whatever response your body makes. Once you have identified an emotion and physical sensation, go on to the next step.

Step Two: Go outside in nature. Go out into a natural environment and find a place to stand. Climb to the top of a hill, if possible. Ideally, stand barefoot to connect more directly with the landscape.

During a trip to Peru, my group was visiting Ollantaytambo, a citadel in the northwestern end of the sacred valley. Atop the temple of the winds, we completed this powerful exercise as a group. There is power in numbers when harmonizing with the elements. Plus, the group was winded after the steep climb up more than 200 rock stairs at 9,120 feet above sea level; all stale air was excreted from our lungs when we began clearing our energy fields.

Whether solo or in a group, begin by connecting with the forces of nature that surround you.

Step Three: Wind breathing. Stand with your back to the wind. Inhale a deep breath of wind, and feel it expand in your lungs and move down into your belly. As you exhale, remind yourself that breath is a personal wind that connects us with others; your wind is capable of reaching the other side of the world in a matter of days.

Continue your wind breath until you feel calm and connected with the world around you. Visualize roots extending from the soles of your feet, burrowing into the ground below. Connect these roots to a flowing underground river. As you exhale, allow the wind to pull the cleansing water up into your body and wash away any blockages you encounter. Once you feel connected, call upon the winds of spirit, using the following prayer.

Begin by thanking all the people who have contributed to your life. Be grateful for your joys, challenges, and sorrows. Invite the rivers, streams, rocks, trees, fire, mountains, and the forces of the wind to be present with you. Ask for clarity. Then say . . .

> *Winds of spirit, enter this sacred space-time*
> *continuum that is my life.*
>
> *I call upon the rock people, the rivers, the streams,*
> *the mountains, the star people,*
>
> *grandmother moon, grandfather sun,*
> *and all the elementals.*
>
> *Come to this sacred ground. Be here with me now.*
>
> *I call upon the winds of change, the winds*
> *that are older than the caves,*
>
> *the first winds that moved all of creation.*
>
> *Eurus, Notus, Zephyrus, and Boreas,*
>
> *I invite you to come from each cardinal direction*
> *to watch over my landscape and me as I do this work.*
>
> *Come here now to help me clear any heaviness*
> *in my heart, body, and soul.*
>
> *I am in awe of the wind.*

Step Four: Wind Wash. Stand with your knees slightly bent and arms extended to your sides, as far as you can comfortably reach. Begin by turning to face the wind. If you are unsure which way the wind is blowing, or if there is only a slight breeze, look for subtle clues: fluttering leaves on a tree, birds flying, swaying blades of grass, or the movement of air on your cheek. If in doubt, listen to your intuition.

As the wind begins to blow, whether gently or forcefully, visualize it unwinding the tension as it spins in a counterclockwise direction. Pay close attention to the places in your body where you feel anger, frustration, sadness, disappointment, and stress. Imagine the wind capturing the energy from these pent-up places and carrying them away high into the sky, where they can no longer be seen, heard, or felt. Feel the wind pulse through your body, removing any unwanted energies from your body.

Turn and face the opposite direction, and repeat.

Continue until you feel the denseness completely leave your body. Ask that any energy that is not yours, or any energy that is not in your highest and best good, be lifted from your energy field. Command these energies to return to the wind as a clear pure wind surrounded by love.

Step Five: Seal your cleansed energy bubble. Using your hands, seal your energy bubble. Begin with your left hand on your pelvic bone and your right hand on your coccyx (tailbone). Then sweep both arms upward and outward toward the top of your head, inviting in a fresh wind while creating a sphere of protection around your body.

You will know you've achieved your goal when you begin to feel lightness; a smile will appear and you'll start laughing and/or dancing as the pain subsides. Suddenly, the wind will stop blowing and you will feel peaceful, joyful, and fully present. This is wind magic.

More pronounced symptoms require stronger winds. Keep in mind that stress has a cumulative effect. You may need to repeat this exercise several times depending on the nature of your situation.

Step Six: Say a closing prayer. Once you summon the winds on your behalf to engage wind work, you need to thank them and send them merrily away. Otherwise, you run the risk of the winds wreaking havoc in your mundane life.

Winds of spirit,

Breath of all life,

Please forgive me for anything I may have said
or done to call this disruptive storm into my life.

I flow gently with the winds of change.

Eurus, Notus, Zephyrus, and Boreas, thank you.

The wind blows where it will.

I am in awe of the wind.

CHAPTER 14

WIND KNOTS:
MANAGING INTENSITY

"I'll give thee a wind.
Thou art kind.
And I another.
I myself have all the other;
And the very ports they blow,
All the quarters that they know
I' the shipman's card."

— *MACBETH, I*[1]

The proper art of tying knots to control weather dates back to the 13th century and is attributed to the wizards of Lapland, the witches of Shetland, and the Isle of Man.[2] To ensure the weather would work in their favor, sailors purchased magical knots from wind witches. These potent charms were used to command the wind. Magicians gathered winds from mountaintops, entrapping varying intensities into knots. During an expedition, a sea captain would untie a single knot to call up a gentle breeze, two knots for a half gale, and three to summon a storm.

New England sailors had a similar practice: they tossed silver coins overboard to regulate winds. Much like us today, sailors were not always adept at calling up the perfect wind to suit every situation; sometimes tossing in too much silver raised a powerful storm, causing their boat to capsize.

For eons, humans have attempted to control nature. Wind spells have been cast for blessings and by sorcerers to cause harm. In Greenland, women were said to be capable of raising storms following childbirth, in an effort to beckon their husbands home promptly to meet their newborns. Ulysses received his winds in a leather bag from Aeolus, king of the winds.

As you become proficient at knot making, you will learn how to use wind knots to harness your thoughts, your emotions, and physical objects. Your knots will become sacred containers of stored energy.

The following exercise is best performed on a beach or atop a mountain, although it can be done almost anywhere outside, as long as a breeze is blowing. You can work in a group, but each person's knots should be hidden from others' so you can focus intently on your own knots. There is an unspoken law of attraction that states that for our prayers to be answered, we should offer them up to the wind in a sincere manner. The same goes for your wind knots. In the olden days, knot makers would protect their sacred knots by covering them with their hands, in the same way a storyteller would shelter "his flame from the wind."[3]

Tools Needed: A piece of rope or cord, and winds of varying intensity. You will need to mark one side of your rope with a colored string, paint, or marker, so as to differentiate between each knot.

Step One: Opening ceremony. Find a comfortable place to sit, like a rock or tree stump. Begin by tuning in to the forces of nature. Inhale a deep breath of wind. Feel it fill your lungs and expand into your belly. As you exhale, remind yourself again that your breath is capable of reaching the other side of the world in a matter of days. We are all connected through our breath, the wind.

Begin your knot ceremony with a wind invocation, a prayer thanking all the people who have contributed to your knot, all the knot makers who have come before you, the plants that have offered themselves to the rope, and the rivers, streams, rocks, trees, fire, and the winds that are older than caves. Ask that each knot be tied at the perfect moment. Ask for guidance to remind you to release them at the divine moment, and only for a sacred purpose. Be mindful to pray for other people with their permission and a clear heart.

Step Two: Tying the first knot. Begin by tying an overhand knot. Take your piece of rope, form a loop, and pass the other end through the hole. Repeat the following words: "I command the power of the wind to be placed into this knot for safekeeping." Like a surfer, wait for the perfect wave. When the energy of the breeze feels right, finish the first knot by securing it firmly, but not so tight that it can't be untied when needed.

Step Three: Tying the second knot. Continue your connected breathing. Prepare the second knot and wait for a second, stronger breeze. Repeat Step Two.

Step Four: Tying the third knot. Repeat a third time, this time waiting for an additional wind to blow.

Step Five: Give thanks. Once you have completed your three knots, thank the ancestors for showing you the ways of this ancient wind practice. End by saying, "These powerful knots have been worth making."

Step Six: Storing your knots. The power of the coiled knot is proportional to the strength of the wind that you placed inside with your intention and prayers. Coil the wind knot counterclockwise and store it in a safe place. Draw upon the power of the knot whenever you need to regulate the intensity of wind in your life. To release the wind, simply uncoil the rope. Untie one knot if you need to get your energy moving forward, untie two when you need a strong push, and release the last one when you are ready for a complete upheaval.

One wind believer experienced the thrill of untying her second knot prior to taking a licensing exam. Her first knot provided support for a family trip. After unleashing the power of her second knot, she finished her exam in record time and was awarded a state license. Since the first two wind knots had produced the desired results, she decided to loosen the third knot, hoping to eliminate an unhealthy habit. However, at the mere mention of the third knot, other aspects of her life quickly unraveled, catching her by surprise. She quickly retreated from untying the third knot and placed the wind knots back on her altar for safekeeping.

One time I untied the third knot and, within days, I lost my job, which led to me needing to move several states away. In retrospect, I see that this disruptive event was divinely orchestrated. Nature has its own sense of timing and consciousness. Winds blow of their own accord, when and wherever they choose.

Chapter 15

Cooperating with
Your Inner Winds

Once you have established a practice of praying, meditating, and grounding on a daily basis, you will be ready to call upon the inner winds for soul support and guidance.

It is important to remember that these beneficial winds have endured throughout history. My phenomenological research and group study have shown that these deities teach you how to cooperate with change, while not necessarily supporting your desired results.

The morning after the 2016 U.S. presidential election, upon learning the outcome, I went to my altar to pray for guidance. My community was in a deep shock. After praying, reflecting, and meditating, I pulled a winds of spirit card. It was Mari, the divine wind goddess of the Basque. The message was, "Know that you are held by the divine." When Mari blows in from the caves of northern Spain, it is a signal that Shakti energy is omnipresent and flowing. She arrived as a soothing wind goddess from the south, to help me transcend my disappointment. The south is about needs, desires, and emotions. While I was studying her qualities earlier in the week, I realized that my vision was limited by my own desire for a woman in the White House. Even though I felt the populace ship was off course, I understood, that there were divine, invisible winds at play.

To put their power into perspective, these winds of spirit witnessed and participated in the creation of the earth hundreds of millions of years ago, long before the advent of human beings. These spirits have been working in the universe ever since the beginning of the earth's timeline, when the first act of creation was caused by the movement of air. These wise winds of spirit have reappeared in today's modern world. I believe they have arrived to assist humanity evolve into a higher state of existence, which the Vedic traditions call the Sai yuga.[1] They are here to help us reestablish our divine connection with nature. This transition out of the darkness requires a massive shift in the collective human consciousness. The annihilation of old, worn-out ideas will create a fertile earth where we can plant spiritual seeds of truth. Working with these inner winds of spirit can provide you with inner peace no matter what storms may be brewing in the outer world.

Engaging the winds of spirit for personal healing is not for the faint-hearted, nor is it for those who want to remain sleeping. To put this concept into context, think back to a night when you were awakened by a vicious screaming wind. The branch tapping against your window represents the unceasing thought patterns that create turmoil in your consciousness. It is during those scary moments that you how learn to navigate or patiently wait out the storm. Once you step upon the path of awakening, you realize that the inner winds of spirit cannot be controlled. Their purpose is to offer you divine guidance and teach you how to cope with change.

I invite you to approach this work with respect, and with the sole intention of waking up from the illusion in order to be of greater service to humanity. Early on, members of my Facebook Wind Believers group learned it was not prudent to invite in a different wind each day. During a seven-day challenge of inviting in a new wind of spirit daily, we recognized the need to take a day off. Everything was shaking up in my life, at work and at home; by day three I was exhausted. After that experiment, I began to call upon a weekly inner wind instead of evoking new energy daily. I would also open to any page at random, whenever I needed an explanation of current events.

As you become familiar with the qualities of each wind, you can summon one or more at will. For current weather trends, you can randomly open a page in Part IV to receive immediate insight and guidance from a wind god/goddess. (To gain deeper insight and wisdom, I encourage you to study the processes in Chapters 11 and 12). Each wind deity detailed in this section has his/her own unique story. As you read through these stories, you may feel a resonance with certain deities. Make notes of your daily experiences as well as your dreams. Over time you will begin to understand and even recognize these subtle energies as they move through your life.

CONJURING AN INNER WIND

Step One: Go outside, or open a window to allow fresh air to flow into your environment.

Step Two: Get centered and grounded. Take three deep wind breaths. Exhale any expectations you might have for the day, and inhale new possibilities.

Step Three: Open any page at random in Part IV, and read the accompanying story to receive the cultural context. As the wind moves up from the base of your spine and out through the top of your head, ask the wind god/goddess you have called upon to fill you with the quality he/she is associated with.

Step Four: Determine which cardinal direction feels most relevant to your current situation, keeping in mind that each direction also contains a crosswind. Being shoved sideways by a crosswind can be beneficial. A client of mine who is often under public scrutiny spent many sleepless nights because of disruptive crosswinds. Once we cleared the air, she realized the importance of sweeping her energy field on a daily basis. We called up Fūjin, whose quality is to *cleanse*. She invited the energy of this wind to flow through her every morning until her sleep patterns returned to normal.

Step Five: Open your body, heart, and mind to the expansive, invisible spirit of the wind.

Step Six: Observe how this wind guides you throughout the day. Call upon this wind as needed throughout the day. Watch for synchronicities.

Step Seven: At the end of each day, it is important to thank the wind for coming, and to *set it free*. This is true even if you are working with the same wind for an extended period of time.

CHAPTER 16

REMOVING
RESISTANCE TO CHANGE

Your body is a map to the secret treasure chest of your awakening. As you integrate wind wisdom into everything you do, navigating through life becomes a study of experience from which you can make the best decisions from a place of stillness. The following is an exercise for pinpointing the exact location of a single issue in your life. This exercise builds upon the wind breath exercise, working with an inner wind, finding your current coordinates, and clearing resistance to chart a new course of action. Please carefully read through these steps before beginning.

Step One: Wind invocation to open sacred space. Begin with a wind invocation, as previously explained. The sensation of a breeze indicates the presence of spirit. You are ready for the next step.

Step Two: Ask yourself, "How do I feel?" Identify anything that is disrupting your peace of mind, thoughts, feelings, needs, desires, bodily pain, loss, and disconnection. State this out loud or silently to yourself.

Step Three: Scan your body. Start with your feet, and move slowly up your ankles, toward your calves, thighs, abdomen, solar plexus, shoulders, arms, throat, and head. Identify the places in your body where you feel resistance.

Step Four: Open to an inner wind god in Part IV of this book to facilitate your healing.
The inner wind god to help you today is _____ .

Step Five: Anchor yourself in Mother Earth with your wind breathing. Stand with your feet shoulder-width apart, with knees slightly bent. Close your eyes and breathe the air deeply into your belly. Invite the emanating force of the wind god/goddess you chose to help with your healing.

Step Six: Find your cardinal wind (see page 127). In order to fully understand your current situation, you need to know which quadrant of the map your cardinal wind is coming from. Imagine you are standing in your favorite spot in nature. A path stands before you, and as you walk up this path, take note of which direction you are heading—is it north, east, south, or west? Make a mental note of which direction you are headed.

Step Seven: Ask the wind to heal you. Visualize _____ (the wind you have selected) rising in your body, beginning at the base (your feet) and moving upward. As it moves, clear all blockages. Focus your attention on the places where you felt the energy was stuck or where you felt pain in your body.

Ask the wind for advice. What was the thought, feeling, body discomfort, or disconnection about? Wait for the information.

Then continue with your wind breath to propel the blockage from the top of your head. Extend this wind breath out to the universe, and become the witness to your debris as it propels outward to the heavens and stars. Offer it to the solar winds. As you exhale, envision your breath as a wind that releases negative emotions, blockages, and unwanted thoughts. Open your heart and mind completely, and surrender to this experience.

Step Eight: Second scan. Scan your body a second time. See if there is anything more for the wind to release in this session. Then close the space. Use your hands to seal off any energy that no longer belongs to this time-space dimension from the solar winds.

Step Nine: Ask for a new vision. Once you have cleared, ask the wind god/goddess to provide you with a new idea, thought, emotion, feeling, or spiritual guidance. Wait for the answer. You may hear it, think it, smell it, and intuit it. Trust whatever comes.

Step Ten: Make notes, a reminder that healing occurred. Which wind god/goddess came to help? _____.
What quality did they bring to your healing? A client of mine who was in a whirlwind felt absolute stillness when calling upon the wind. There is an abundance of information in every experience.

Identify the quadrant that the cardinal wind blew in from and record its theme.
Direction: _____
Theme: _____

This will provide greater insight. For example, if you experienced a pain in your knee connected to the east, it might signify that your thoughts are resisting new beginnings. In the south, your emotional responses to a situation may be rigid, causing you pain. In the west, you may be trying to carry a burden alone, causing added stress as you walk. The north implies unyielding beliefs in the divine winds (grace) that may inhibit spiritual growth.
What is the new thought brought in by the wind?
Survey your surroundings, inhale the aromas, feel the sensations, and listen.

Step Eleven: Release your wind bubble and close the sacred space. Wind work is sacred. Therefore, you should have an intimate and harmonious relationship with the wind and nature. You just said this. As the story goes, he realized that next time, using a nickel would suffice. This same principle applies in your life; one situation may require the soothing winds of a lullaby to lure you into a peaceful slumber, while during times of stagnation, a hurricane-force gale may be required to get you moving forward. No matter which cardinal wind god shows up in your meditation, be like the captain and remember to express your gratitude.

Once your meditation is completed, send the winds back to the four corners of the earth.

With the proper tools in hand, it is time to venture deep into the cave to explore the inner winds. Part I presented an overview of wind wisdom, the basic components of wind meteorology, and how they can help you safely navigate the trials and tribulations of daily life. Part II explored the enduring cosmology and structure of the cardinal winds. Wind wisdom is a perfect blend of ancient principles and modern-day tools. In the next section, you will meet 29 inner winds. Although there are many more, these are the specific winds that revealed themselves to me during the past four years.

Part IV

THE
INNER
WINDS—
FORCES OF
NATURE

INTRODUCTION TO THE 29 WIND GODS/GODDESSES

"A looking glass can be both a mirror and a window."

— GLORIA DURKA[1]

This section describes 29 ancient wind gods/goddesses that have played significant roles in various cultures and religions throughout human history. These unique winds transcend time and space to intersect with your life. Each one has unique powers and characteristics. Once you understand their significance, you will be able to call on them anytime to help you safely navigate the trials and tribulations of daily living.

There are many ways to use this section. You can open any page at random for reference, or undertake one of the many exercises throughout this book to experience the winds in a personal manner.

Suggested practice is to form your question, take three deep breaths, close your eyes, and open any page in Part IV. Read the complete description for each wind to gain insight as to how it may be influencing your thoughts, feelings, and actions. Some winds may feel familiar, while others may seem like distant shores.

As you become familiar with the qualities of each wind, your heart, mind, and soul will gradually open and be enriched by the grace, wisdom, and guidance each one has to offer.

AMAUNET (EYGPTIAN)

Obscurity

Call to this Egyptian goddess to hold space for
obscure wisdom and creative energy.

Amaunet, whose name implies *hidden one*, is a mysterious, primordial feminine wind deity. As the North African queen of the Lower Nile, she represents the invisible dual aspect of the creative process. The earliest indication of this mother goddess of wind dates back to the Old Kingdom in Egypt. Hieroglyphic shards dating back more than 3,500 years portray her wearing a red crown, with a winding serpent around her body, which is the Egyptian symbol of divine authority.

Women of the ruling class held immense power during the early days of Egypt. They held prominent government positions, owned land, kept slaves, testified in court, conducted business, and engaged in important ceremonies and rituals.[1] Inscription evidence shows that status was determined by class, not gender.

Amaunet had a male counterpart named Amun. Together, they were regarded as the unseen protectors of the pyramid texts that revealed and communicated the will of the divine to humanity.[2] The pyramid texts found in the temple of Hermopolis provide insight into Egyptian cosmogony. There were several creation stories about the dawn of ancient Egypt. In one particular version, there was the Ogdoad, which consisted of eight primordial deities: four pairs of gods, each with a female and male counterpart. This expression explains the dual nature of existence: light and dark, cold and hot, etc. These natural states were not metaphors; they represented the cosmic forces through which life-giving energy is manifested.[3]

According to this myth, in the beginning there was the primeval ocean; Naunet/Nun, chaos; Kauket/Keku, darkness; Hauhet/Hehu, formless; and Amaunet/Amun, an unseen dynamic force of nature. In many myths, Amaunet is referred to as the feminine aspect of the creator god, Amun (his wife, or consort). However, some earlier texts describe Amaunet as the mother goddess who did not need a father to conceive, and might have been the first life-giving god. Amaunet breathed life into the nostrils of all lifeless matter, and then took responsibility for preserving her creations.[4]

The movement of air (wind) in the dark abyss brought forth time, giving birth to everything else that exists within.[5] Time was measured in units of kingdoms, with several hundred years spanning each major period. By the end of the Old Kingdom, Egyptians worshipped many anthropomorphic gods/goddesses. Over the millennia, pantheism replaced polytheism, Amun was elevated to the solar god status of Atum-Re, and Amaunet's position was diminished.

When Amaunet breathes new life into your consciousness, be prepared for a divine revelation.

EAST

Obscured meanings arrive upon the words and breath of the dawn wind. In the Old Kingdom, the word *priest* meant she/he who "carries the papyrus roll"; there were magical powers in the divine words.[6] Many hieroglyphics show women offering prayers and performing rituals. This may be the perfect time to begin a writing project and share your message with others.

If you are struggling, Amaunet can assist you. Consciously place your awareness on the essence of your breath and thought. Watch as words shift in and out of your mind. Do not look for meanings; the answers you seek lie waiting in the gaps between your thoughts. Reflect on the wisdom of these spaces before making a decision or beginning a new project.

SOUTH

The breath of life nourishes your heart. Inhale deeply as you enter into the domain of sacred time, the place of nothingness, where all potentiality resides. As the sun rises, imagine the radiant, healing light of Ra (sun) fusing with the the wind power of Amaunet. Allow this energy to flow into your third eye, and flood your entire body. Daily morning rituals such as this one, or simple ones such a reciting a prayer, can improve your emotional well-being. Write down your intentions in a journal or on a slip of paper. This, in and of itself, is an act of devotion. Amaunet connects you with the divine, revealing the hidden truth in your emotions.

If you are feeling dried up, visualize the red color of Amaunet's crown. Ask her to help you to awaken the latent creative potential residing deep within you. This may require a journey into the shadowy side of your emotions, deep inside the womb of your creative heart.

WEST

When she arrives as a hot, parching wind from the west, Amaunet offers you the safety of a secure womb to restore your physical energy. You are likely to undergo an initiation during this period of withdrawal.

If you are unable to find the wisdom in loss, offer a ceremony to the deceased. These can be people, places, or things that no longer have any value in your life. Call upon Amaunet to soothe your soul as you grieve. Dance in the wind, and experience the boundless freedom residing between grief and joy. Wisdom will be revealed.

Egyptian peasants endured a life of labor. If you are working too hard, and obtaining few results, call upon the cosmic energies of Amaunet to help you till the land. She will appear as a powerful protective bull. Enjoy her earthly gifts, especially life-sustaining water. Call upon her for if you wish to improve your health.

NORTH

Amaunet may arrive as a hawk to bring forth knowledge from the ancient mystery schools. She was called upon by new kings to provide them with the esoteric wisdom needed to rule wisely. Arriving from the north, she is reminding you to set aside time and space to perform a ritual (symbolic act that will connect you to the divine): wind invocation; releasing ceremony; or food offering to the nature gods. Whenever you see a flag fluttering in the wind, you glimpse the ways in which all of humanity is moved by invisible yet life-sustaining forces.[7] Cosmic energies are at play when Amaunet arrives from the north. Focus your attention on this timeless wind that propels "itself without end or beginning."[8]

If you are feeling lost, call to Amaunet and ask her to help you find a quiet space. Always keep in mind that all things are connected through the breath of this wind goddess.

BIEG-OLMAI (LAPP)

Signs

*Invite Bieg-Olmai when you are unable to
properly interpret the signs of change.*

The stretch of land above the Arctic Circle covers Finland, Sweden, Norway, and parts of Russia. Relics of Lapp shamanism date back from the first century BCE. When lingering darkness accompanied by subfreezing temperatures prevailed across the mountainous and desert terrain, and unceasing winds howled outside the sod hut, it was essential to be in harmony with nature for survival. Nature determined the flow of time for ancient Laplanders; the slightest changes in the winter-spring air compelled the reindeer herds to migrate to the calving grounds before the terrain melted into slush.

Materials used to assemble Laplanders' drums hint that these nomadic arctic reindeer herders existed close to the end of the late Stone Age.[1] A central figure on every drum was Bieg-Olmai, also known as Bieka Galles. In Scandinavian mythology, Bieg-Olmai held the winds captive in a subterranean cavern. He is depicted holding a shovel in his right hand, used for scooping the winds into the cave. With his left hand, he uses a club to drive them out again to enliven and freshen the breath of the land. To calm a storm, the shamans (Noaidis) would offer up a shovel to appease this fierce god.

When Bieg-Olmai uses his shovel to release the wind from below the snow, it is time to deepen and enhance your relationship with magic, the natural rhythms of your own life, the soul of your surroundings, and the cycles of nature. Call on Bieg-Olmai when you need quiet and want to harmonize your surroundings, and if your metaphoric boat is about to capsize at sea. Invite Bieg-Olmai when you are unable to properly interpret the signs of change.

EAST

The Lapps migrated from east to west. When Bieg-Olmai blows in from the east with a stinging cold blast, your forward movement comes to an abrupt halt. Bieg-Olmai asks you to carefully observe the subtle signs of nature and wait for the perfect moment to act.

Examine your beliefs regarding time. Are you in harmony with the seasons/cycles of your life, and with your natural surroundings, or is your day scheduled weeks in advance, with little regard for daylight? Does your cell phone determine where you go and how you live your life?

Take a break, turn off all electronic devices, and align yourself with the winds of change swirling around you. Take a moment to listen to the story of your life, reflected in the natural world in which you live. Wake up with the sun goddess, thank the man in the moon, listen to the birds, feel the wind, watch and listen for a signal from nature before proceeding.

Whenever reindeer encounter a headwind, they change direction. When a wind blows against you, it may be time to alter your course. Be alert and pay attention, lest you miss a great opportunity. Become a wise spiritual tracker and follow the reindeer.

SOUTH

The arrival of Bieg-Olmai as a fresh, coastal summer wind means that now is a good time to pray and get your emotional house in order. Use the penetrating light of the midnight sun to cast a shadow so you can examine your shortcomings.

A *sieidi* is a sacred Sami space used for personal ritual, where it is possible to communicate with the spirits. Construct or renew your *siedi*; power builds when we return again and again to our place of prayer. Create a ritual to deepen your relationship with your inner emotional winds. Call up Bieg-Olmai to help you harmonize your relationships with others.

Make a power drum and paint it with your personal symbols. The reindeer-skinned drums of the Lapp were used to record personal and communal history. The precise placement of symbols on the drums told individual stories and described the cosmology of the nomadic tribes. The paintings varied with each location and family, but common elements included a central sun separating a horizontal division for the summer and winter camps, plus three vertical levels of experience: sky, terrestrial atmosphere, and underworld.[2] What will your symbols say?

When the wind man ceases to blow in your emotional life, it means you are not paying attention to important signs in your life. You have lost your bearings and need to recalibrate your inner compass. To answer questions, the Lapp would place a copper ring on the membrane of their drums. Using a reindeer horn beater, they would strike the drums, and when the ring came to a natural resting point, they would have an answer. Look for reoccurring patterns in your life, and you will find the answers to your questions.

WEST

The Sami Noaidi believed that people have two souls, an animated soul and a "free soul." Using a specialized drum to help them gain access to other realms through trance states, shamans tapped into the free soul for ethereal travel, which allowed them to communicate with invisible spirits. The Noaidis were the intermediaries of the gods, usually called upon during periods of famine, sickness, or while hunting. Access your inner shaman by entering a trance through meditation, dance, or by drumming. Ask the spirits to help you harmonize with the elements in your surroundings.

Are you feeling wind-slapped? The Sami were necromancers who used their skill to harness the wind into knots for sailors. You learned how to adjust your wind knots in Chapter 14. Bieg-Olmai might blow in as a harsh wind or an early frost if you're not paying close attention to your family and community. A home was one room, with a central kitchen where friends and family gathered to share food, drum, and sing. Open your heart; call upon the local winds to remove any negativity or blocked energy from your home or office, and bring harmony into your personal relationships. Spending time with children will help you remember and appreciate the importance of storytelling and the value of simplicity.

NORTH

When Bieg-Olmai, the Samek wind man, arrives from the north, it is time to pause. Enter into his eerie silence. Explore the haunting majesty in the field of snow trees. The powerful soul of nature will transcend your perception.

Ask a question, and then use your drum to travel inward and climb up the mountain to the precipice of your rich spiritual center. Become like a Sami observer who can perceive the age and intrinsic quality of snow. Deconstruct your spiritual beliefs according to color, size, temperament, texture, and age. Alignment with your natural world is necessary if you wish to read and interpret the signals in your life properly.

The wind man will capsize your ship when community values are neglected and replaced by self-serving dogma. Enter the dark cave where the winds are stored and you shall find the truth. Make a sacrifice and reconnect with your spiritual self. Inspiration will rise like a glorious waning spring sun, growing ever brighter as you serve the needs of spirit and strengthen your bonds with family, groups, and community.

CARDEA (ROMAN)

Facilitator

*Call to Cardea to close doors on the past, and
to open the doorways of new opportunity.*

Roman farmers had a god for every occasion. During the seventh century AD, rituals were conducted at home in simple, round straw huts, while elaborate temples, designed exclusively for the gods, were erected throughout the land. During this time, women called upon the goddess Cardea to bless their homes and families. They hung wolf fat on metal hinges and wool wrappings on wooden doorposts as a means of protection from the menacing spirits of the night.[1]

Originally, Cardea was a nymph who was committed to virginity and nontraditional patriarchal marriage, until an enamored Janus, the ancient Italian god of doorways, tricked her. Cardea would flirt with suitors by enticing them into an empty cave and asking them to wait for her. Once they entered, she would flee. With keen eyes on both sides of his double-faced head, Janus did not succumb to her wiles, and he seduced her. In exchange for her love, Janus elevated her to the status of the white goddess, the overseer of hinges, and the four directional winds. He also granted her dominion over the flowering hawthorn, which was used to protect homes and children.

Doorways were therefore regarded as guardians that bore witness to possibilities and dangers. Ritual practices organized around farming communities were rooted in obligation to the clan. Gates to the city remained open except during times of war. As the goddess of hinges, Cardea was the axis upon which seasonal winds revolved; she possessed the power to unlock mysteries and reveal possibilities.

Once a year, during the Feast of Cardea, the head of every household enacted the ritual of tossing beans into the dooryard as a plea for redemption. Beans were the symbol of prosperity, alive with the spirit of Carna, who, according to legend, may or may not have been Cardea. The passing of gas was considered a good omen. A strong breeze crossing your doorway assured divine protection. According to the poet Ovid, call upon Cardea "to open what is shut, to shut what is open."

EAST

Cardea swings the door of fate wide open when she arrives as an east wind. Be prepared to experience life anew, while undergoing abrupt changes in your daily routines, habits, and rituals. As the goddess of hinges, Cardea stimulates and awakens the potential in your life by bringing unseen forces to the forefront and making them visible.

A door slamming shut is a powerful message to seek opportunity elsewhere. Everything in nature has a time, a reason, and a season. Don't expect to harvest a bountiful crop from a fallow field.

SOUTH

When Cardea blows in from the south and greases the hinge of your gate, you have won the favor of the gods. The white goddess has brought your needs and desires to the frontlines of experience. The doorway is open for closer connections, kinship, and affection. Cardea's sweet breath brings change and opportunity into your life. When summoned, she is a fierce protector of children, as well as your inner child. Accept her guidance and express your gratitude by placing flowers on the windowsill of your home.

The struggle for existence was always at the forefront of Roman society, and the needs of the community were of primary importance. Cardea reminds you that you are never alone; your friends or blood family can fill an emotional gap. Remember to put the needs of others before your selfish desires.

WEST

Inus Geminus is a double-gated Roman temple, with one door facing the rising sun, while the other looks toward the setting sun.[2] As Cardea blows in, she closes both doors, vanquishing what no longer serves your best interests.

When you cling to old lifeless forms, Cardea arrives as anger, disappointment, and heartache. Resentment leads to physical deterioration and illness. Ask her to blow the past away. Be sure to close all doors that remain ajar.

NORTH

When Cardea descends from her castle in the stars and blows in from the north, pay close attention to her prescient messages. Inspiration is achieved through sacrifice, discipline, and dedication to community. In order for your crops to germinate, grow, and thrive, your cauldron of inspiration must nourish the community. When faith is strong and judgments are few, enlightenment can be found in ordinary experiences and is available to everyone. Cardea reminds you that there is no separation between work and worship. Cardea can be a strong wind, slamming doors, creating havoc and confusion. You can appease this tumultuous wind with an offering of selfless service to your community.

DOGODA (POLISH)

Compassion

Request Dogoda's help to neutralize highly charged situations.

Much of what was previously known about Old Slavic religious practices (pre–966 AD) came to us in bits and scraps via the early writings of the Romans, Greeks, and Arabs. From these old documents, together with current research and the Internet, it is possible to piece together the significance of these legends, songs, proverbs, and exorcism practices.[1]

To ensure their survival, it was common practice among old Slavic shamans to offer sacrifices to the harsh nature spirits. One practice produced thick clouds of smoke to drive off evil weather spirits, and there were rituals performed in honor of the Big Dipper to mark changes in seasons.[2] While Dogoda was not considered a major god in these shamans' history books, he was the only directional wind they anthropomorphized, expressing the qualities of love and compassion. His appearance ensured that the corn would grow and the mating season was in full bloom.

When the predicated belief of the people is that everything in the world is infused with God, and God infuses everything with God's own unique spirit, it makes sense that the countryside of Poland is dotted with sacred landmarks. The Polanians pray at crossroad shrines, holy wells, at the wooden groves at the base of giant boulders, and at cairns for direct contact with the divine. The Slavonic tribes of the field worshipped Mother Earth, Matka Syra Ziemia. Trees, rocks, and animals were considered older than mankind, far wiser, and were consulted for aid and advice.[3]

While Dogoda blows in from the island of Buyan as a gentle wind god of compassion, you may be requested to explore the concept duality in your life; everything that is not of love may need to go.

EAST

Tradition is the bedrock of the Polish people. Ritual preparations leading up to an event are key; Christmas Eve has long been a primary celebration. When Dogoda blows from the east, sacred memories are being stirred in the depths of your subconscious, in order to shift your beliefs. Loyalty to time-tested strategies will help you navigate change. Examine the signs and omens that cross your path. Although the loss of an idea, a loved one, a job, or a life pattern may leave you feeling sad and disappointed, take heart in the knowledge that Dogoda's breath will warm your cracks and crevices with the winds of compassion. Remain true to your rituals and ceremonies.

If you are prone to seeing the world in black and white, Dogoda reminds you to take note of the various shades of gray that are also aspects of your life. Clear your mind by discarding old ideas. Dogoda may manifest as strong words from a loving friend, reminding you to stay present with your current course. This is a time to energize sacred practices and let go of preconceived notions and expectations.

SOUTH

The arrival of Dogoda in the south signifies that this is the time for a moral victory over your emotions. Dispel whatever is ugly; lighten up, laugh, and enjoy yourself. Repressed emotions may be triggered by an unexpected loss, recognition, achievement, or illness. With Dogoda's assistance, you need not suffer needlessly. You can experience compassion for yourself and others whilst moving toward a satisfactory resolution.

Do not become a martyr to your pain. You do not have to fight to stand your ground. Dogoda can help you loosen your grip on current survival strategies that no longer work. Dogoda may cast a spell of heartbreak to expedite the healing of old wounds and enable you to soar like an eagle.

WEST

When Dogoda comes from his home in the west, show respect for your spirit visitor by setting an extra place at the table. Allow your dreams and visions to take precedent over the mundane world. Be on the lookout for omens.

One Polish myth describes how the nation of Poland was founded. An army troop stopped to rest in a meadow alongside a lake, when they noticed a large eagle circling overhead. It came to rest briefly on the edge of a cliff and, as it spread its wings to soar once again, the rays of Dazhbog (the sun) struck its wings, which made them glitter like gold. Taking this as a harbinger from the sun god (Svarog), Lech, the leader of the battalion, declared this place their new home, calling it Gniezno (the Eagle's Nest). To this day, Gniezno remains the historic center of Poland. This myth is a reminder to keep your inner and outer ears and eyes open for signs that will guide you to your rightful place.

Despite harsh and impoverished living conditions, the Poles remained true to their faith. When Dogoda blows open your doorway of doubt, enter with joy, confidence, and an open heart. Be grateful for all that you have, large and small, and remember to share your gifts with others.

NORTH

Polanians paid homage to a supreme God, while beseeching numerous nature gods for help and guidance in their everyday lives. Dogoda comes bearing the gift of compassion. Reconcile your idealistic beliefs and allow others to express themselves as individuals. Dogoda blows in from the north to remind you to put away the sword of your own illusions. Things are not always as they appear.

Symbols may not always be what they appear. For example, the swastika originally represented the poles of the Big Dipper constellation, as well as time itself, which, according to shamans, moves both forward and backward for Polish-speaking pagans. However, the Nazis redefined the swastika to symbolize destruction and war. To understand this idea fully requires that you undergo a paradigm shift of consciousness. Put aside preconceived ideas.

Dogoda comes as a reminder that sacred time is circular, and that events that occur in the past are directly influenced by present actions. Offer up your devotion to the wind and stars, and perhaps you will change the course of history.

EHÉCATL (AZTEC/MIXTEC)

Passion

Arouse Ehécatl when plans have turned to ashes, when you feel heartbroken, or when you are ready to call forth your beloved.

Ehécatl-Quetzalcoatl (Ehécatl) is the Aztec god of invisibility and intangibility who oversees the mysteries of passion and love. Aztec cosmology is built on the premise that there are five suns. Each sun represents a different era with its own creation story in which humans are born, sustained, and destroyed by the elements of nature (earth, wind, fire, water, and earthquake, respectively). Ehécatl is one of the many faces of Quetzalcoatl, the famed feathered serpent deity. In Nahuatl, Ehécatl means *four winds*, referring to the four cardinal directions.

Ehécatl presided over the second sun of creation, called "Four Wind." During this period, human beings fell from the grace of the gods and, after 364 years, were destroyed by a hurricane. As Ehécatl blew, he swept away the debris, and those who survived were transformed into monkeys. Ehécatl reappeared in 1427 AD during the dawning of the fifth and final sun. According to Aztec legend, Ehécatl traveled deep into the underworld and persuaded Mictlantecuhtli, the god of death, to give back some ashes and bone. Ehécatl mixed the bone with blood from the gods and created humanity.

Ehécatl also snuck into the lower world, abducted the maiden Mayahuel, and brought her to the middle world. Their passion was so great that they became one and merged into a single tree. Upon awaking from sleep, Mayahuel's elder Tzitzimitl journeyed to the middle world, pulled the lovers apart, shredded her granddaughter into pulp, and then returned Ehécatl to his rightful place in the wind. Whenever the wind blows, the Aztec believe it is an expression of Ehécatl's desire.

In order to fully understand adult love, one must experience loss in a personal manner. Seeds of passion grow from the embers of disappointment, and later blossom into fragrant spring lilies. Like the wind, love, passion, and relationships are mysterious forces. If Ehécatl appears in your life, a wonderful surprise is stirring in the chaotic ashes of your subconscious self and will soon manifest in your life.

EAST

If Ehécatl appears as a longing eastern wind, it is time to listen closely to your heart. New projects, new lovers, art, and/or music will ignite your passion.

When he arrives as an adverse windstorm, be prepared for the removal of worn-out love stories and soured memories preventing you from experiencing a new cosmic order in your life. It is time to examine your beliefs regarding love.

SOUTH

Ehécatl is fanning the flames of your innermost feelings and hidden desires. Until you are willing to risk your heart, love stands at bay. Remember you are worthy of love and passion. Allow the mysterious thread of the universe to carry you into the next cycle.

Unlike Ehécatl, who was molded from a stone knife, you are an emotional being who thrives on love. A howling Ehécatl is prompting you to open your heart to love. A wind stirs deep within you, asking you to soften your heart and forgive those who have harmed you. Now is the time to heal the emotional scars left behind by abuse, loss, or abandonment.

WEST

Ehécatl brings the rains to nourish your crops, signaling the end of the dry season. Wash away your inhibitions and rejuvenate your body with physical activity. Celebrate with dancing, hiking, gardening, swimming, or sex.

When Ehécatl opposes you by offering you forbidden fruit, be alert and cautious. The sun may set on your goals if you merge with the wrong energies, as in the tale of Ehécatl and Mayahuel.

Misguided passion and intrigue might pull you from your true path, if you do not establish clear boundaries. Ask Ehécatl to help you to sweep away any blockages that stand between you and a bountiful harvest.

NORTH

When Ehécatl blows in from the north, it is a sign that invisible forces are at work in your life. A soul mate needn't necessarily be your lover; it is someone who has your back, no matter what troubles you may face. Enrich your life by connecting deeply with the people you love, and with those who have your best interests at heart.

When inconsistent forces abound, Ehécatl points out that you are neglecting your daily rituals, which prevents you from keeping your spiritual life in order. Ask Ehécatl to help you understand the deeper aspects of your true self. It might be something as simple as rearranging your altar, planning a vacation, or going on a spiritual retreat.

ENLIL (MESOPOTAMIAN)
Destiny

Request Enlil to help you align with your
hidden forces of fate and fortune.

The ancient Sumerians occupied the southeastern region of Mesopotamia (now Iran-Iraq), meaning "land between the rivers," in reference to the Tigris and Euphrates. This fertile crescent of land, located in an arid desert, was ideal for agriculture and home to a great civilization. The Sumerians made supreme advancements in the use of language, writing, mathematics, architecture, astronomy, irrigation, and property ownership.

According to ancient mythology recorded on cuneiform tablets unearthed in the Mesopotamian region, before the advent of civilization chaos and darkness ruled the universe. During the first century BCE, exalted gods of nature were personified to bring harmony to planet Earth. An (the sky) was the supreme deity of the heavens. Together, An and Ki (Earth) gave birth to Enlil, the executive ruler of air. Enlil (Lord Air) was the supreme deity and chief of the gods, who granted fates and kingships. The half-bird, half-human lord ruled over agriculture and oversaw all social conventions.

The firstborn son then separated his parents; An parted from Ki and laid claim to the heavens, leaving the powerful Enlil to rule the atmosphere, while his younger brother Enki was charged as keeper of the waters. The separation of elements caused personified gods to rise from the primeval mud and prepare the earth for human activity. The first humans were created as slaves and made to perform the work of the gods, who had grown tired of tilling the land with Enlil's hoe.

Each human community had its own ruling god, appointed by the all-powerful Enlil. He administered *earthly law,* decrees from the gods that outlined social structure and duties. Admirable traits included war and destruction, implying that for better or worse, all human behavior was divinely inspired. Unable to live up to his own standards, Enlil was banished to the underworld for committing rape, which fathered the concept of good and evil. Humans stopped living in harmony with nature, overpopulation occurred, and according to the favored historical text *The Epic of Gilgamesh,* Enlil caused a great flood that destroyed civilization. It was Enlil's supreme duty to decree all fates, and his commands could not be overturned.

When Enlil casts a storm from his sacred temple *é-kur* (mountain house) at Nippur, you can be certain that the winds of fate are at play in your life.

EAST

As the keeper of the *Mes,* Enlil blows in from the east to give you an insight into your destiny (*dharma*). Allow the invisible winds of Enlil to enliven the fires of your divine imagination and steer you in the right direction. Just like the ancient creation myths, do not readily accept things at face value. Question authority whenever new information is presented.

When embarking upon a new journey, or when starting a new enterprise, the forces of nature can be chaotic. If Enlil appears ready to flood your new venture, this suggests that old thoughts and ideas must be destroyed before new possibilities can germinate and grow. There is divine timing behind all events.

SOUTH

The arrival of Enlil in the southern quadrant is a reminder that you were born with free will, and that the choices you've made in life have brought you to where you are today. Enlil stirs your karmic emotional patterns, which are important markers of time, each one containing a jewel of wisdom. Once you develop the skills needed to navigate your inner emotional windstorms, you will be able to navigate safely toward your goals.

The presence of Enlil as a raging storm indicates supreme judgment of self and others. Needs and desires are neither good nor bad, so step back and observe your expectations objectively if you want to grasp their true significance.

WEST

Enlil was banished to the netherworld for raping his consort, the young grain goddess Ninlil. As a result, the cycles of the moon were created. Just as Ninlil remained faithful to Enlil and followed him into the darkness, you are reminded of your own shadowy aspects. Utilize the magic of Enlil's hoe to till the soil and unearth the answers you seek. Facing your own shadow will lift you from a world of darkness and allow you to shine the light of love and compassion upon yourself and others.

If Enlil arrives as a side wind in the west, death is imminent. This might be the demise of a relationship, a project, an idea, etc. Remember that death invariably leads to the birth of something new. New skills must be acquired before entering the next cycle.

NORTH

The appearance of Enlil as a north wind indicates that invisible spiritual forces are at work in your life. It is time to trust in the power of the divine. Know that Enlil protects your destiny, which you will attain when conditions are ideal.

Unexpected upheavals may beset you if your spiritual practices are not aligned with your river of destiny. When Enlil appears ready to submerge your ideals, ask yourself:

- "Where am I attached to my vision of reality?"
- "How can I be of better service to my life's mission?"
- "Am I taking nature for granted?"

By restoring order to your rituals, your beliefs will become aligned with your destiny and success will surely follow.

ESAUGETÚH EMISSEE
(MUSKOGEE CREEK)
Protection

Invoke the master of breath when a new idea or creation needs protection to germinate, or you need shelter from chaos.

The Muskogee (Creek) people lived in communities composed of matrilineal clans. In this society, clans were named after the elements and denizens of nature—Wind Clan (Hutalgalgi), Bear Clan (Muklasalgi, Nokosalgi), and Bog Potato Clan (Ahalakalgi), to name a few.[1] Elder clan mothers oversaw the well-being of the tribe, along with their eldest brothers, who maintained law and order, land division, marriage, war, and justice. Rabbits, waterfowl, and other animals played a vital role in the retelling of their myths.

Muskogee legend encompasses the stories and rituals of many different tribes that occupied the southern states of the Americas long before they were recorded by European settlers in the 14th century AD. Remnants of these earthen pyramids have been found in the southeastern states of Alabama, Georgia, and northern Mississippi dating back to at least 700 AD.

There were several different creation stories, including that of the Muskogee (Creek), who apparently traveled east from the Rockies to escape the Great Flood. At the end of the Great Flood, Esaugetúh Emissee climbed to the top of a great hill, Nunne Chaha, in the middle world. As the waters began to recede, he placed moist mud into his hands, breathed life into it, and shaped it into human form. Since the land was mostly covered by water, it was the master of breath's job to protect the mud people by constructing water channels and stone-walled mounds. He is the Supreme Being, Hisagita Misi, "the one who is breath" and "makes Indians."[2] The sound of his name represents the movement of breath from his mouth.[3]

In that time, everything in the universe was equal. There was no judgment day, reward, or punishment. Sins were forgiven during the annual Boosketuh (Green Corn Festival). Those who practiced these traditions were cared for by Esaugetúh Emissee at the time of their earthly transition, while those who behaved poorly were left to find their own way home along the Milky Way.

When Esaugetúh Emissee blows away the fog in your life, it's time to bring awareness to your creations and realize that you are shaping your destiny; protection and care are required.

EAST

Windstorms of greed brought the Great Flood, which destroyed almost everything on the earth's surface. As the water receded from the land, the playing field was once again cleared, allowing humanity to start anew. When the life-giving breath of Esaugetúh Emissee arrives in the east, you are being offered an opportunity for a fresh start, such as a new job, a new relationship, a change in residence, or an improvement in your health. A powerful breath may arrive as a precognitive dream, offering insight into a new beginning or new ideas, or as a piercing wind of change that levels your foundation. Trust that what you are shaping and manifesting in your life will be supported and nourished.

If you are overthinking and feel overwhelmed, call upon the master of breath to help keep your head above water. This wind offers protection as you build a new foundation. It may be time to renew or replace your guardian spirits, power animals, and healing tools.

SOUTH

Your interchange with the wind of spirit, Esaugetúh Emissee in the southern quadrant indicates that a purification ceremony is required to help strengthen your inner walls, as you navigate your way through emotional waterways.

Each year the Creek atone for all their actions by working at the central fire and performing the stomp dance. Clans gather early to prepare for the renewal ceremony; during the week they work, pray, dance, fast, and cleanse in the river. During the dance ceremony, all offenses are excused, except murder and rape. It is time to prepare for your own renewal. Intention is key to your success. Plan your own ritual and gather friends, your four-legged familiars, and healing tools to ensure success.

If you are holding on to the past, this disruptive power may rise within you as a reminder that everyone deserves a second chance. If Esaugetúh Emissee appears in a dream as sadness, it signals a time when grieving is necessary before you can move toward your fortune.

WEST

All creations rise from the earth in the east. Esaugetúh Emissee blowing in from the west signals a blood death; it is a time to let go and realize that death is like the setting sun. Forgiveness allows you to reconnect with family and friends.

If ornery winds cross your path, it is time to release possessions or energy in order to restore balance. Acts of cleansing can include smudging, taking a salt bath, or dipping into a cold mountain stream. It is time to restore balance in your life.

NORTH

The Creek cosmology is based on duality; the body is animated with a vital force and intertwined with its soul counterpart.[4] Esaugetúh Emissee comes to remind you that there is no judgment day, and your soul spirit can fly free as the north wind. You can take these spirit flights in ceremony, during dreaming, and when you exhale your final breath. If you live your life in selfless service, Esaugetúh Emissee will guide you through all transitions.

Ask yourself, "Am I striving for the highest ideals? Are the choices I make best suited for the good of the whole?" Like the plains people, we must consider how our actions affect our community.

Esaugetúh Emissee assisted and protected humans who took the right action, and left others to fend for themselves.[5] Take time to consider what relations are in your best interest, and don't be concerned about what is right or wrong. In life there are no good decisions, bad decisions, or absolutes. Some actions may bring you closer to your intended harbor, while others might lead you astray.

FENG PO PO (CHINESE)

Harmony

Call Feng Po Po into action when you seek
to balance the forces of nature.

Feng Po Po appeared as the primordial goddess of wind and storms in China during the Han dynasty, dating from about 200 BCE. Exact dates and details are sketchy since most records in China, including the Book of Documents, were burned during the rule of the first emperors.[1] Many goddesses/gods grew out of animism, shamanism, divination, and geomancy. Oracle bones found at the Shang dynasty capital, Yin, date from 1,300 BCE.[2] Feng Po Po, also known as Madame Wind, is the crone. With her age comes the wisdom that in harmony all things are possible.

Often depicted as old and wrinkled, Feng Po Po rides on the back of a tiger with a goatskin sack of wind in her arms. On calm days this wise woman shows her generous spirit by balancing the elements, but when her mood turns foul, she releases the pent-up winds and creates storms. Like Feng Po Po's bag of changeable wind, the idea of balance implies that two prevailing winds must always be present (yin and yang). Yin and yang seek to explain the complementary forces of nature: dark and light, cold and hot, female and male, negative and positive.

A light breeze is a welcome addition on a hot summer day. A mood can be a foul wind if we work too hard and don't allow time for rest and relaxation. To be fully human is to live a balanced life of giving and receiving, work and play, love and loss. Balance is a virtue, as an excess of anything, no matter how good, can become a vice. When Madame Wind gusts into your life, it is time to ask where you are in harmony and service, and where you are not. Perhaps you are abusing power and on the verge of collapse.

EAST

Feng Po Po arrives to shake the foundation of your beliefs. Examine which opposing thoughts need harmonizing, so you can move forward. Contemplate Confucius's ideal of ignoring the two ends, and take the middle path. Contradictory thoughts can be held simultaneously. For example, you may want a relationship but also want to be single; you may enjoy the freedom of a child, yet be a responsible adult; and you might want to lose weight while craving ice cream. Your ability to unify ideas will enable you to make better choices and improve your life.

Polarized thinking can add power to your thoughts. Decision making requires the ability to weigh different options and outcomes. When Feng Po Po comes as a disruptive force of nature, it is time to seek balance. Are you practicing mindfulness daily? An ancient Buddhist concept states that if you are too busy to meditate, you need to sit for a longer period of time in order to achieve spiritual balance.

SOUTH

Feng Po Po blows in as a breath of fresh air to offer emotional support as you harmonize your relationship with nature. Venture into the forest and fret not; Madame Wind will safeguard your unfinished projects during your absence. Restoration and cooperation are keys to your emotional health. This is not the time to overcommit.

If you feel like you are giving too much of yourself to others, it is time to retreat. Join Feng Po Po and her tiger on a magical ride into the dark, rich underbelly of your soul. Uncover the benefits you receive from unhealthy codependency, like not having to take personal responsibility for your actions. Strive for interdependence. Guilt does not serve you.

WEST

Every life cycle and project consists of a beginning, a time of preservation, and an end. Madame Wind arrives as a forceful west wind to create havoc and remind you that collapse is imminent. In youth our bodies are resilient and we feel invincible, but as we age we become wiser and the choices we make become paramount. Conserve your energy. Call upon Feng Po Po to help you simplify every aspect of your life. Reduce stress by eating better and living within your financial means. Strive to find balance and restore your natural rhythm.

When Feng Po Po arrives as a devastating storm wind, it is a stern message to stop meddling with nature and the affairs of others. Do not interfere with the harvest; decomposition is part of the natural order. Focus on clearing your own field.

NORTH

The spirit of community is a foremost concern of the crone. Yin and yang are complementary elements of nature. The Feng Shui compass predates the written word. Feng Shui (literally *wind water*) was a tool devised to keep humanity aligned with nature. It is believed that these energies of wind and water contain an invisible chi, and when balanced, these animated life forces benefit our health, our home, and the community at large.

The arrival of Feng Po Po as a gusty dark north wind signifies that something important is about to be revealed. Trust your inner compass to lead you like the south-pointing compass led the ancient ones out of the fog. Integrity is a key principle for reconciling differences in the community. Are you using your power of prayer for self-service, or for the betterment of your fellow neighbor? The best way to remain balanced is by giving to others unconditionally.

Magic and power can be deceptive winds. Beware if Feng Po Po arrives as a stormy wind. Throughout China's long history, dynasties collapsed whenever power was misused, and so it is with circumstances in your life.

FŪJIN (SHINTO)

Purification

Request Fjin, the "Prince of Long Breath," to cleanse the air, provide stability, and nurture your personal growth.

According to the 1,300-year-old Kojiki (Record of Ancient Matters), civilization came into being millions of years after the formless chaotic universe was initially created. Finally, at the end of seventh epoch of gods, Izanagi-no-mikoto and his spouse, Izanami-no-mikoto, were granted the power to create the Japanese archipelago. As they stood above the chaos upon heaven's rainbow (a floating bridge), they used a jewel-encrusted spear to pull the 6,852 islands out of the swirling waters. Next, they created their home of heavenly pillars, followed by eight major nature deities, including Kami-Shinatsuhiko-no-Mikoto: the wind.

Legend states that when the couple gave birth to the wind deity, Kami-Shinatsuhiko-no-Mikoto, his forceful breath dispersed the clouds that had covered the planet since the beginning of time, which allowed light to illuminate the world. In Japanese culture, masculine and feminine deities were often complementary aspects of the same Kami, and over time they shape-shifted into a new identity; Kami-*Shinatsuhiko*-no-Mikoto (Kami-*Shinatobe*-no-Mikoto, feminine version) became the horned, fanged-headed Fūjin.

The relationship between myth and real life is complex, and in Japanese culture, origins are unquestioned and unquestionable.[1] On the surface, they do not believe in superstition, yet today, mythical deities remain front and center as guardians of their numerous pillared temples. This unspoken mythology flows continuously throughout the chain of islands that comprise the nation of Japan.

Fūjin may arrive as a dark cloud in your life and manifest as unspoken emotions from another person, or as a force of nature.

EAST

Growth, abundance, and prosperity are assured when Fūjin arrives as the god Rajin (the god of thunder), who disrupts your calm with a thunderous squall. Once the rain subsides and the clouds part, your path will become clear. Now is the time to "act as if you believe," no matter what illusion nature holds before your eyes. Like the sacred isles of Japan, everything is connected; seeds carried on the breath of a wind are nourished during a rainstorm and thrive as they grow in the nourishing light. Now is the time to expand your knowledge. Take time to read a book, sign up for a workshop, or attend a class.

If you feel torn apart by a raging storm, like the scattered islands of Japan, now is the time take to examine your beliefs, thoughts, and actions and connect with the heavenly rainbow bridge of authority.

SOUTH

Partnerships are at the forefront when Fūjin arrives as a disheveled *oni* (ogre), with Rajin. With a booming clap, he stirs your deep-seated need for intimacy. This is not a time to talk things out; instead, spend some quiet time with a loved one, sharing feelings and thoughts you both cherish.

If a dissident wind disturbs your peace, it may be that a touch of vanity has blinded your vision. It is easy to misinterpret signals that pop up in daily life. Are you projecting your feelings onto others? Before responding, ask Fūjin to guide you on a cleansing inner journey. Forward movement naturally follows noble thoughts and kind feelings.

WEST

The arrival of Fūjin in the west calls for ceremonial behavior. The primordial mother, Izanami, died when giving birth to fire and was sent to the land of Yomi. A heartbroken Izanagi pursued her to the land of the dead, where he spied her charred, maggot-eaten body. He fled and tried to block the passage to the underworld with a boulder. Izanami cursed the people with a plague, and to offset her curse, Izanagi gave birth to a new human being every time he bathed. If you are experiencing a loss of any kind, performing a physical cleanse will help you establish balance in your life.

Fūjin brings attention to your breath when he arrives from the west. Fresh air is essential to good health. It is time to breathe deeply, fertilize your body with nourishing food, and get plenty of exercise. Desired results are obtainable when this divine, benevolent wind is at your back.

Fears that have lain dormant for years rise from their slumber and shake the very core of your foundation. Physical aspirations may seem distant and feel like the snowcapped Mount Fuji, perfectly shaped yet difficult to reach. Disruptive forces of nature are gifts that can stir your inner winds and get you moving forward on your path again.

NORTH

When the fertile wind of abundance arises in the north, it is a reminder to tend to your spiritual obligations. Sacrifice has roots in the premise that if you give in a sincere manner, the gods will reciprocate with a gift of equal or greater value. Offering a gift to spirit is a gesture indicating that you are respectfully moving into prayer.

Japan is known as the country of eight million gods. In the Shinto tradition, everything in life is filled with spiritual energy. Fūjin may appear as a storm-creating demon when you act selfishly by taking more than you give. Everything arrives in the proper sequence; reflect on the divinity of nature to bring balance, calm, and harmony into your life and the community in which you live.

HOLLE (TEUTONIC)

Mystery

Summon this mysterious benefactor to provide solace when you have lost a loved one. The goddess can bless the birth of an idea, enterprise, or a child.

Holle comes from the German word *kind*. This powerful goddess is as mysterious as the bog in northern Germany that is said to be her home. She is linked to many goddesses: Herke; Perchta, wife of Woden; Holda; Holl; Hulda; the queen of heaven; and Mother Mary.[1] She plays a prominent role in German mythology, fairy tales, folktales, customs, and taboos. Scholars have long debated her history and importance, while Jacob Grimm dates her appearance back to the first century AD and tells us the legends of Holle have been found in France, Switzerland, Austria, and the Czech Republic.[2]

Before the emergence of central halls for prayer, ritual and ceremony occurred in nature. Her famous ritual site remains intact to this day. It is located near a swampy meadow called Frau Holles Pond, high in the Meissner (Meißner) range's east–west Germany border. Rivers, streams, bogs, and wells led to the other world where "Our Lady" is said to move unhindered on behalf of human requests.

Most agree that Holle was a sky goddess who worked in the realms of light and darkness. She traveled great distances by cart to intervene in the world of human activity. Women prayed to her for fertility and longevity by bathing in the waters at the entrance of the Hollenstein cave. Her vast wind power extended to bringing the birthing souls of children from the watery depths of her bogs. Christians regarded her as the queen of witches who carried unbaptized children in her wagon as she journeyed throughout the Milky Way galaxy.

In Germanic ideology, this generous mother is known for being stern, but always fair. Hard work is rewarded. Laziness is not tolerated, and severely punished. In one legend, Holle arrives as a blustery wind and knocks on a farmer's door. He welcomes in a stray dog left stranded in the cold. One year later, Holle returns as another menacing storm to thank and reward the farmer with gold for treating her dog with compassion.

What makes Holle stand out as a wind spirit is her airy nature, an amalgamation of different cultures, religions, and schools of thought. She appears across northern Europe as the leader of the Wild Hunt. In Norway, she is known as goddess of fertility and health. In Roman lore, there are similarities between Holle and the Lady of Abundia (Abundance) and Satia (Fullness).[3] Over the millennia, her appearance has been cited as ugly, beautiful, malevolent, and good.[4] These disguises and her ability to shape-shift have contributed to her mysterious invisibility.

Her patronage includes whirlwinds, snowfalls, fertility, and the souls of children. This wind goddess generates fiery ethers that fuel the central hearth. Fire is integral to sustaining life, and whenever smoke mingles with Holle's sacred breath, the soul of a community ignites. Holle's myth lives on in present-day Germany; whenever snow falls, people say, "Holle is cleaning house and shaking the feathers out of her comforter."

When Holle flies across the sky after emerging from the dark depths of the water, she brings new life. A benefactor has arrived, and you will be rewarded for your honesty, generosity, diligence, and sincere efforts.

EAST

Now is the time to clean house and get your affairs in order. Take comfort because the feathers from Holle's trembling quilt will provide adequate protection until the time is right to launch your new project. Offer Holle a bouquet of flowers and she may reward you for your kindness.

If Holle appears as a menacing eastern wind, be forewarned: a test of your humanity is likely. Scrutinize your motives. You must find peace and harmony before you can proceed.

SOUTH

Something hidden will be revealed. Discipline and hard work are required, which will lead to accomplishment, contentment, and reward. Maintaining an attitude of gratitude will win Holle's approval every time.

It is time for a ritual cleanse. Take a salt bath and release all negativity and discord from your life. According to lore, women would travel to Holle's pond high in the Meissner Mountains, where they would bathe before sunrise to ensure that their requests were answered. Call upon the queen of the sky to restore peace and joy.

If Holle arrives as a stormy wind, you are being put on notice that selfish behavior will not be tolerated. Your task is to transform this behavior into a gift that will benefit others. Holle is capable of transforming gold to dust in the blink of an eye if she detects a greedy heart.

WEST

If you desire a child, or something new to be birthed, call to this goddess; her powers are heightened on May nights (May Day Eve) and Christmas Eve, when she is prepared to fulfill your wishes. Holle will intercede on your behalf, whether you are planning a journey or harvesting your crop. If you are willing to put forth a sincere effort, Frau Holle can teach you how to magically transform common flax into the finest linen.

When Holle blows in as a western wind, your patience may be tested. You will not be rewarded if your crop is disheveled. Holle prefers cleanliness and order, so don't be surprised if she challenges you. Yield to her wisdom and she will lift you from chaos and restore peace and harmony in your life.

NORTH

As leader of the Wild Hunt, Holle chaperoned the procession during the winter solstice. Celebrations and rituals were held in her honor, especially on New Year's Day and in May.

It's time to celebrate. Holle is rewarding you for your hard work and charitable actions. Frau Holle bestows a spiritual gift of precious jewels in your life when she appears as a northern wind.

If you have failed to consider the heart of your community, you may experience a long, cold night of the soul, as Holle rushes in like a whirlwind and drives her cart over your best-laid plans.

ILMARINEN (FINNISH)

Inventor

Conjure this innocent wizard wind
for prosperity, magic, and alchemy.

Magic is the key ingredient in this epic tale of a people who lived along the coast of the Baltic Sea, in the northwestern corner of Russia. Finno-Ugric mythology endured the test of time, recorded by Elias Lönnrot, a physician, botanist, and mystic scribe in 1835. For 15 years he traveled both sides of the Ural Mountains and recorded the rune songs of the shamans. Before these ancient mysteries were scattered by the wind, Lönnrot published the "old" Kalevala in 1835, hoping to resurrect the collective cultural memory of the Finns.[1]

At the core of the 22,795 mystical verses in the Kalevala are two creator gods who happen to be brothers. Väinämöinen is the wise shaman, and Ilmarinen is the innocent wizard craftsman. As the perpetual old-man bard, Väinämöinen's powerful chants and songs bring the enemy to tears, bring quiet stormy seas, and give warmth to the sun.[2] Ilmarinen is a supreme deity of divine origin who created the sky, and the son of the celestial Ilmar, who was impregnated by the wind at the dawn of creation.[3] Throughout this epic tale, these two brothers continually act in complementary ways.

In one tale, Väinämöinen encourages Ilmarinen to conjure a sacred Sampo, wooing him with the promise of marriage to the beautiful and mysterious rainbow goddess. Despite his skepticism, Ilmarinen journeys north from the Land of Heroes to the harsh barren lands of the Lapp witches. Possessed by a fairy maiden's charm, the alchemist constructs a smithy on a colored rock, igniting a raging inferno from which he extracts a plethora of objects, including weapons of war that he immediately destroys. After four failed attempts, Ilmarinen calls upon the four winds for assistance. The Sampo appears in the flames as a mill with a multicolored top, capable of grinding out grain, salt, and gold.

Despite producing a generous dowry for the queen of the Lapp witches, the toothless queen hid the Sampo under nine rocks and refused to let her daughter leave Pohyola; and despite his ability to manifest tools magically from clothing and bend iron with his bare hands, Ilmarinen was deemed lacking in matters of the heart. However, later in the Kalevala, the suitor returns and wins the daughter's hand after completing three challenging tasks: plowing a field of vipers, muzzling a bear and wolf, and capturing the monster pike in the underworld.

When Ilmarinen "sets the four winds blowing" in your life, the magic of alchemy is at play; yet be wary, for the gold may be otherworldly and different from what you expect.

EAST

Until the Kalevala was restored as their national tale, the Finnish people had long forgotten their origins. When Ilmarinen fans your fire, it is time to extract the truth from the brightly lit flame of the smithy residing within you. It is not enough to craft your identity from illusions, social media, or television. Immerse yourself in the deep waters of your divine inner wisdom. Great inventions are like cloths woven from the threads of innovative thoughts and ideas.

Have you forgotten the words to your favorite childhood song? Hum until the words rise up from the depths of your history. Become a fascinated seeker; search for words while you sleep and explore the worlds of magic within your dreams.

SOUTH

Don't be fooled when the billowing warm air of Ilma wafts through your open window. Even though Ilmarinen may blow in from the south as a compliant and passive wind, he is a persistent force of nature. Keep in mind that after he wooed and wed the fairy maiden, he carried her home to the Land of Heroes to create a family. It is time to let go and create a sense of belonging in your life.

Stand upon your epic story and shed the drama of your past, so that you may heal. Let the warm winds of Ilmarinen show you how to shift your consciousness from that of victim to hero.

WEST

When Ilmarinen ushers in mysterious winds from the west, partnerships with family, nature, and community are at the forefront. You are reminded that although supernatural rituals might produce immediate results, these gifts are not always in your best interest. Money and magic do not necessarily produce happiness. Sorrow is a process that a wizard's magic cannot heal. The best inventions are gifts that serve the community at large. Prosperity flows freely when your intentions are pure and kind.

Broken hearts can lead to selfish motivation, if left unchecked. The beautiful object of Ilmarinen's magic was cold, heartless, and unmoving. Eventually, he returned it to the fire and wisely fashioned millions of beautiful stars to illuminate the night sky.

NORTH

The cold northerly winds lured Ilmarinen to the dismal swamps of Lapland. In order to fulfill his dream, he left the comfort of his home to face death-defying challenges, including two journeys into the underworld. These can be seen as symbolic. Ask your inner shaman to help you discover your origins and reclaim your soul, as well the soul of your community. As the protector of travel, Ilmarinen will guide and protect you as you venture within and back.

Only by cooperating with the forces of nature will you be able to reclaim your personal power and magic. The Sampo was composed of the tip of a swan's feather, the milk of a farrow cow, the fleece of a summer ewe, and a tiny ear of barley, all of which are symbols of time. Tap into the power of your personal medicine, adorn your altar with sacred objects, and restore your belief in the divine mystery.

KARI (MALAYSIAN)

Expression

Call upon Kari for support
to give voice to your thoughts and feelings.

Many aboriginal races from Africa, India, and Asia settled in the abundant jungles and lowlands of Malaysia before the last ice age. The archipelago, which extends from Burma and Siam to Singapore, was a popular crossroad for east–west trade. The Semang pygmies were dark-skinned hunter-gatherers who carried charms and were always on the move. According to their bamboo records, Kari is one of their three primary deities, who created everything with his word, with the exception of life on planet Earth.[1]

Legend tells us that after Kari directed the Ple' (the mediator between the Supreme Being and other gods and humans) to fill the lush earth with humans, she used his fiery breath of life to infuse their bodies with souls.[2] Souls could travel freely; during dreams, they took on the forms of animals (especially tigers, elephants, and snakes), and upon death, the spirit returned to the creator in the Land of the Fruit Trees.[3]

Kari governs self-expression as the ruler, judge, and controller of invisible winds. These traits are invaluable when negotiating trade and spirits in the magic arts. In his book *Pagan Races of the Malay Peninsula,* Walter Skeat says the Semang have an animistic theory of the universe that consists of methods by which the soul (the vital force of gods, humans, animals, vegetables, and minerals) may be influenced, captured, and subdued by the will of the magicians.[4]

Language is at the root of human collective consciousness creation.[5] Even with modern scientific genetic testing, scholars still use ancient symbols, words, and language to connect the human evolutionary thread. Kari arrives as a thunderous wind, a reminder of how the power of language connects you to everything that came before and all that will follow. Like the wind that makes music when it rustles through the leaves of a tree, our breath creates music when it is forced through the reed of a clarinet, or across the opening of our lips as we speak. This kind of friction relates to the energy of Kari, which teaches us to create something beautiful from life through verbal expression.

EAST

A change in self-expression is inevitable when Kari shows up in the east. Now is the ideal time to forage the jungle for new ideas and modes of communication. Think like a nomad as you make this transition, and gather the right number of roots, tubers, and fruits from the past so you can move forward with ease. Kari arrives as an ally, ready to help. He gives voice to your ideas, feelings, and desires through story, dance, and song.

Kari may arrive as a rebellious storm. Keep in mind that memories are stored in the east. To move forward in life may require adaptation and mental dexterity. Once you have given voice to outmoded thinking and discarded stale ideas that are weighing you down, ask Kari to carry them away.

SOUTH

Although you may feel frantic when Kari blows in from the southern quadrant, it is important to remain emotionally centered, calm, and balanced. Emotions may be raw, leaving you feeling exposed, covered only by a bark cloth. Take daily walks in nature, exercise, and seek wise counsel. If you surrender to the energy and wise counsel of Kari, you will learn how to "go with the flow" and adapt to change. Savor the sweetness of the ripe, low-hanging fruit of the jungle.

Be mindful of the words you speak when conflicting emotions run high. Words can be like bows with poisoned arrows that leave indelible scars and permanently damage relationships.

WEST

Kari arrives as a wild western wind of self-expression. His presence may conjure up ghosts that are better left in the past. Take time to discern whether your current creative expression merits a fertile garden plot or should be discarded like seeds in the jungle, left to regenerate on their own.

Nomads were constantly on the move, and found shelter under overhanging rocks and leafy trees. Movement can be stressful, creating wear and tear on your body. Are you flexible? The Semang were easily able to climb tall, thin trees because of their flexible limbs. What mechanisms do you have at your disposal for coping with physical limitations? Kari reminds you to take care of your body; it is a sacred vessel that offers safe passage to your intended harbor. By surrendering to the energy of change, you will be able to expand your range of motion.

NORTH

Kari brings collective wisdom from the north. Without the community's expressed agreement, your projects lack soul energy. Cooperation is the key to harmony and a door to wisdom. New opportunities waft from the thicket when you are willing to negotiate and compromise with others. The landscape may appear as a jungle or a rugged mountain peak; but with collective support, community survival is guaranteed. While the chief of the tribe was often the shaman or medicine man that went first, he was not above anyone, as everything and everyone is equally infused with Kari's breath of life.

Whenever you need guidance, know that the wisdom of Kari is always yours for the asking. Celebrate by performing a ritual dance, and sing your song of pain and joy with a passionate refrain. Do you have a magic charm? Learning to ask for support during times of hardship will lessen your load, increase your vitality, and allow you to move forward with confidence and joy.

LA'AMAOMAO (HAWAIIAN)

Ancestor

Assemble the winds of La'amaomao to enhance vital relationships.
La'amaomao can help regulate the force and intensity of shifting winds.

The *mo'olelo* is a sacred story used to demonstrate the dynamic life force between the Hawaiian people, their language, and the world of nature in which they lived. According to *The Wind Gourd of La'amaomao,* all the winds of Hawaii were once contained in a supernatural gourd.[1] The *calabash* (gourd) served as the intermediary between its keeper and the 32 winds that originated at the horizon, in the *rua matangi* (wind pits).[2] Pāka'a inherited the wind gourd from his mother, La'amaomao, who was a descendant of the wind goddess bearing the same name. When chanting and removing the *tapa* (bark cloth) from directional holes in the gourd, Pāka'a could invite hundreds of South Sea islands to trade winds for protection, bountiful harvests, and rain.

During the 16th century AD, Pāka'a was the chief navigator and trusted servant to King Ali'I, Keawenuiaumi, the chief of Hawaii.[3] Pakaa enemies within the king's ranks convinced the ruling chief to grant them authority. Defeated, Pāka'a sailed from the island of Hawaii with the *calabash* containing his mother's bones and waited patiently with his son Ku-aPaka'a at the bay of Kolo (near Hikauhi) for his revenge.

Years passed before King Ali'I, Keawe-nui-a-Umi was fully aware of his staff's deception, all the while missing his faithful servant. After a series of dreams revealing Pāka'a's location, the king's entourage set out to find him. Ku-aPaka'a sailed out to greet the fleet. His father, Pāka'a, was hiding in the bow of the boat. He encouraged Ku-aPaka'a to engage Chief Keawe-nui-a-Umi with riddles and wind chants in order to lure his boats ashore. Upon dismissing the young man as nothing more than a distraction, the crew convinced Keawe-nui-a-Umi to head back out to open sea. Trained by his father to be adept at summoning the winds, Ku-aPāka'a unleashed powerful storms from the gourd of La'amaomao. Many lives were lost before the defeated crew limped back to shore. Pāka'a succeeded with his well-executed plan to punish his enemies, and gained the respect of his Ali'I, Keawe-nui-a-Umi.

If the winds of La'amaomao, the sacred *calabash*, are stirring in your life, you are being called to examine your past, present, and future relationships with people, places, and things in all areas of your life.

EAST

When the twisted *tapa* emerges from east hole of the wind gourd, be prepared to have your mental faculties put to a stringent test. Opportunities disguised as challenging riddles will manifest on the horizon of your consciousness. Use your mental acuity to find simple solutions. Remember that Pāka'a's trials and tribulations with the wind motivated him to invent the sail.

What are you waiting for? Even though Pāka'a believed his king would eventually return home, he wisely spent his time training his son and building a strong community. If the wind brings forth a confusing mixture of bones, uncertainty, or unexpected results, call upon La'amaomao for guidance. Have faith, be patient, and know that a new strategy will emerge to show you the way.

SOUTH

A prevailing wind arriving from the south is a reminder to examine your connections. Islanders know who they are, through their deep connection with the land, air, and sea. Where are your roots? Are you able to name the prevailing winds in your community, or do you take these life-giving forces for granted? Hawaiian locals recite the names of winds and rains as testimony to the sacred elements. On Oahu there are more than 45 winds, each with a distinct name and personality.[4] By yielding to the wise counsel of nature you will be safe, regardless of the emotional upheavals you encounter.

The south wind beckons you to "know thyself." In order to establish a true connection between yourself and nature, you have to experience the elements of your immediate surroundings.

WEST

There is an abundance of natural resources on the land and in the sea surrounding the seven Hawaiian islands.[5] Before contact was established with the outside world, parcels of land known as Ahupua'a were shared by everyone. Each parcel was rich in natural resources and home to elemental spirits. Everyone had access to water, food, mountains, and the ocean. When La'amaomao blows in from the west, you are being advised to exercise *aloha* (love of the land). This is a good time to tend to your garden, stroll through nature, and pay attention to the daily and seasonal cycles. Be kind, be generous, and share your wealth with others.

Take an active role in solving community problems. Take a new step every day; be prudent in your use of water, create less waste, and recycle more often. It is time to remember that planet Earth is like an island, possessing abundant resources and the ability to regenerate when we show respect.

NORTH

As the wind enters your life from the northern side of the gourd, you are being asked to focus your attention on the sacred words that you speak. In Hawaii there are Kapus, which are strict rules for proper behavior. Sacred *mo'olelo* are only told during the daylight hours, and passing before the speaker is insulting to the gods. Tend to your altar; these sacred spots are vortices of energy offering a place of rest and comfort for the north wind. Positive creative energy arises from well-intended prayers, chants, and mantras.

The naming of people, places, and things will provide a sanctified order in your life. A proper Hawaiian introduction includes reciting the family's ancestry back to the original island inhabitant. Native Hawaiians understand their role, function, and position in society by the pronouns attached to their names. Choose your words carefully before opening your mouth. Sharing information may be important, but sharing wisdom will provide inspiration for ages to come.

MARI (BASQUE)

Gift

*Call to Mari three times whenever you are lost
and she will come to your aid.*

Mari is the prominent mythical deity of northern Spain, a mysterious goddess who resides deep in the base of the Pyrenees Mountains. According to genetic evidence, the Basque have resided in the area for more than 9,000 years. Mari's malevolent and mischievous influence has been felt throughout the ages. The Basque people regard her as the source of all creation. Her beauty is as rich as Mother Earth herself. Much like the weather patterns she oversees, her surname and appearance often change. Sometimes Mari appears at Anboto in the north of Spain, bringing wet weather, and then moves on to permeate Alono with her hot, arid breath. She is able to manifest as a woman-tree joining earth and sky, as a bird, or as an elegant woman draped in a red gown as she drives her cart across the face of a full moon. Whenever you need guidance, call to her three times by one of her many names (Andre Mari, Ama Lurra, Old Woman of the Mountain, or Marien Damea) and she will come to your aid.

The cultural origins of the enigmatic Basque language, Euskara, predate most Indo-European linguistic forms.[1] The Basque people consider themselves to be the original occupants of northern Spain. Jesuit priest José Miguel de Barandiaran painstakingly recorded thousands of Basque myths and tales by means of the written word.[2] Singing was as effortless as breathing; thousands of songs provide a glimmering insight into their rich and mysterious legacy.

Goats were used as sacrifices to appease Mari, and while the goat cult was originally organized as an attempt to explain and control natural phenomena, it later became a strong cultural resistance movement that was used to fend off orthodox religions. The Basques were the last pagan strongholds in Western Europe, with only a few converting to Christianity in the late 1600s. Priests allowed and participated in the witches' sabbats (seasonal rituals), held in remote mountainside communities.[3]

"Like many in the world of the old day," witches were a common but contradictory theme, enticing Europeans to listen to carefully crafted tales.[4] And, while you shouldn't believe in them, you shouldn't disregard them either. In those parts, people would always err on the side of caution when approaching Mari's lair, praying for grace outside her cave, not daring to enter, for fear of the cave-dwelling spirits known as the Sorguin.

If Mari casts down a storm from her cave, be assured that a gift is forthcoming. To receive it fully, you will need to coax its essence from the depths of the rich, dark, feminine mother.

EAST

You may feel shaken by the urgency of the wind when Mari plummets from the eastern sky as a fierce ball of fire. Her jolt will stir long-forgotten memories of the magical powers waiting within, as she brings the ageless gift of wisdom. Start by recalling the favorite tales of your childhood. Find the themes of creativity woven within them, for therein resides the mystery of your own soul's calling. As you reassemble your memories, your personal tale of being will be revealed.

Mari brings a gift of contradictions when she side slaps you and bursts into your life like a lightning bolt. She refuses to adapt to consensus and will shake your beliefs to the core. When missionaries encroached her cave, Mari transformed one into a raven who later died from fright. Ask yourself, "Where am I compromising or abandoning my own knowingness in order to follow the herd?" Determine the areas in your life where fear is the prevailing wind, and make the necessary adjustments so you can move forward with confidence.

SOUTH

Like a fragrant perfume gently wafting through the air, Mari drifts in from the south to stir and fully awaken your erotic potential. Mari was an androgynous, passionate lover. Although she had a husband named Sugaar, she also brought willing young village maidens to her cave for extended visits.

Mari is also the mother of balance; her offspring were Attarrabi (good) and Mikelats (evil). Call upon Mari to reveal and balance the themes in your life with your inner emotional winds of need and desire. If you feel emotionally undernourished, seek the companionship of women, or take on a new lover.

When Mari blows in as an arid south wind, your passion may feel diminished and parched. She arrives as the divine mother, bearing gifts to resurrect and nourish you. Visualize her red swirling life force dancing passionately in your second chakra. Call on Mari to remove any emotional blockages preventing self-love, the essential force that nurtures your creative soul.

WEST

When Mari comes calling from the west, she is asking you to sit alongside her on her golden couch. Your attention to detail and devoted practice of your rituals has paid off; Mari is offering you the gift of power. Be mindful of your personal code of ethics as you tap into the powerful waters of the mountain spring. Power expands when used in service to others, and contracts and vanishes with misuse.

If Mari shows up as a raging storm in your life, the gifts she bears may sting. No mortal is allowed to enter her dwelling without permission, as she does not tolerate a lack of respect for other people's property or possessions. Ask yourself if you have overstepped the boundaries of others, acted with greed or malice, or allowed your arrogance to rule. Mari can quickly turn your dreams to coal. Withdraw from her cave using the same path you used to enter; Mari is a stickler for ritual. Once outside, reassess your current situation and search diligently for the gold hidden in the ashes.

NORTH

Mari provides spiritual guidance to help you find your way. She resisted all religious efforts to convert her to others' beliefs, and now her powerful wind offers you warmth and protection within the walls of her sacred cave. Her gift to you is discernment. Examine your beliefs and all the knowledge you have absorbed during your life. It is time to drink heartily from the well of milk and honey that flows constantly below the earth's surface. Quench your thirst and receive the spiritual guidance you need to achieve your goals. The soul is like the wind; it moves however, whenever, and wherever it chooses.

Is there a raven tapping on your window? When Mari blows in as a moist north crosswind, she may disguise herself as a bird to get your attention. When you feel the flapping of the bird's wing and darkness prevails, Mari is inviting you to visit the underworld, which pulses with magic, wisdom, and clarity. Do not be afraid. Visit a well or a cave and speak to the ancestors. Mari's gifts of wonder can arrive in a variety of different ways, so be sure to keep your eyes, ears, mind, and heart open at all times.

NILCH'I (NAVAJO)

Intuition

*This wind can be conjured up for inspiration, organization,
or ritual, and to provide strength when needed.*

The Navajo are descendants of Paleo-Indian hunters from the
Monument Valley area.[1] According to Navajo belief, when the universe was created, the sacred wind Nilch'i entered the darkness of
the underworld. Dark and light wind energy fused, giving birth
to mists of colored lights that traveled upward toward the four
corners of the glittering earthly surface. These events are said to
have taken place approximately 6,000–12,000 BCE, after the last
ice age. Nilch'i breathed life into six mountains, including the
four sacred cardinal peaks that form the boundaries of the Diné
Bikéyah (Navajo landscape). The first Diné (Navajos) emerged onto
the earthly plane after an arduous journey from the Black World
to the Blue World, and up through the Yellow World.[2]

Everything in the Navajo world is alive with energy: "wind
that stands within."[3] While in the West, we use language to
attempt to define and order reality, in Navajo cosmology, the Holy
Wind informs all life. Wind possesses all knowledge, having the
power to inform and order life. It also has the ability to command,
compel, organize, transform, and restore.[4]

The Navajo believe there is an in-standing (soul) wind that
enters our body at conception that stays with us until we exhale
our very last breath. The first wind breath determines our destiny.
For the indigenous people of the plains, words express the energy
and movement of wind. Wind enlivens, organizes, mobilizes, and
transforms everything. Wind influences thoughts and feelings,
helping us to make the best decisions and take the right actions.
Through sacred language and ceremony, wind can dispel darkness

and create desired outcomes for individuals and communities. In order to live in peace and harmony, one must develop an intimate relationship with the Holy Wind.

Nilch'i provides meaning and momentum for your life. Listen closely and make sure you are alert because guidance, transformation, and expansion are forthcoming.

EAST

Nilch'i can arrive as a combative wind, provoking the exploration of new ideas. Be open to all gifts, even those disguised as loss, arguments, and disruptions. If you experience difficulty receiving, become a stage actor. Study your lines and cues carefully, and Nilch'i will guide you swiftly through uncharted landscape.

All things in life are an expression of wind that speaks to all who will listen. If you are unsure which step you should take next, move closer toward the distant hill and listen carefully for the sounds of new opportunity.

When Nilch'i appears as a belligerent side wind, expansive thoughts are forthcoming. By accepting others' differences, you will be blessed with the gift of compassion.

SOUTH

Nilch'i arrives as a blue wind from south, a cunning, competitive wind. Your inner voice asks you to look beyond the surface of people, things, and events; they may not be what they seem. Listen closely to your intuition; do not question your gut reaction. If you have been deceived, study the clever trick closely, lest you be fooled again. A thief can only steal your horse when your back is turned; call upon your inner winds to expand your awareness.

Missed opportunities happen when a door opens and you fail to walk through due to fear. Fear is a counterwind; ask Nilch'i to remove any emotional blocks preventing you from moving forward.

WEST

When Nilch'i accompanies the setting sun, rest and good fortune await you. Good planning and resourcefulness have produced an abundant harvest. You will have ample resources to barter during a lean winter, and will be rewarded for your positivity, courage, and determination.

When Nilch'i shows up as a rebellious west wind, it is a reminder to wait patiently until your crops are ready to harvest. Tune into the in-standing (soul) wind of the land before proceeding.

NORTH

When Nilch'i prevails in the dark northern quadrant, it signifies that a transformation of faith is possible. Reality mirrors language, and not the other way around. The power of wind cannot be accurately mirrored in words, as it is incomprehensible. Faith is an ever-changing perceptible wind. Sometimes it arrives as a gale of uncertainty, at others times as a mother's gentle caress. Wind is a constant reminder that the wisdom of spirit is ever-present in your life. Once you understand wind, you will have access to the cohesive elements of energy found in nature.

Nilch'i, "the holy wind that informs everything," offers guidance to those whose inner ears are open. If you feel discordant, Nilch'i encourages you to customize your prayers. Offer gratitude for the strenuous but important lessons learned during the daily, monthly, yearly, or larger cycles of life.

NJÖRÐR (NORSE)

Prosperity

Hail Njörðr for prosperity and
soft summer breeze to keep you calm.

Imagine a time when giants, dwarfs, wizards, dragons, elves, and trolls interacted with gods, aristocrats, warriors, and peasants. These were the beliefs of Scandinavian Vikings (Danes, Norwegians and Swedes) throughout Europe from 780 to 1070 AD. The traditions of the fiery Vikings have been immortalized in poems, where wars were waged and battles fought using swords and magic. Poets were myth keepers; their stanzas held the records of creation, art, adventure, expansion, community, war, and magic.

The Norsemen were innovative shipbuilders, pirates, merchants, and skilled navigators. They traveled boreal waters and unruly oceans as they expanded their trade routes east to the Black Sea, west to Iceland, and south into Scotland, Wales, France, and England. Archaeologists have unearthed burial sites proving that their clinker-built ships reached Newfoundland five centuries before the arrival of Columbus. However, not all Norsemen were roving pirates who conquered the land and seas; many lived peaceful though physically demanding lives as fishermen, hunters, and farmers.

Njörðr was a Vanir god who calmed the seas and placated fires. He ruled over the summer winds, which allowed skilled sailors to travel by water through glacier passes, using northerly and southerly winds to find treasures far beyond their homeland. Sailors had to be brave; sea travel was a gamble that could lead to treacherous encounters with polar bears, getting stuck in calm seas, being besieged by sudden storms, and other unexpected natural disasters. Yet the rewards of bountiful food, spices, livestock, and trade supplies were worth the risks they encountered. According to the poet Snorri's *Prose Edda*, Njörðr had vast wealth, distributing land and treasures as he pleased. Today, Scandinavians still strive to be "as rich as Njörðr," and he is often offered the second toast at meals, for peace and plenty.[1]

When Njörðr blows through your life, your waters become energized and invigorated, signifying that it is time for extraordinary expansion and growth in your life.

EAST

Blowing in from the east, Njörðr offers a bounty of innovative energy. In order to expand trade throughout Europe, the Vikings built elegant, innovative wooden ships that resembled royal yachts. These marine vessels were great technological advancements during the dark ages; they were fast, shallow, able to avoid icebergs, and could also be used as rowboats whenever the seas were calm. Now is the time to venture forth fearlessly into unexplored seas with your innovative ideas. Like a Viking ship, your ideas need to rise above the sea like a glacier and extend beyond the status quo. Enlist new solutions in preparation for those future times when the wind will cease to blow.

If Njörðr blows in as a strong, unpredictable headwind, grab your oars and start paddling with gusto! This is not the time to give up on new ideas; perseverance and hard work are required if you truly want to succeed.

SOUTH

When Njörðr makes his appearance in the south, you will become aware of the polar opposites residing within you. In Scandinavian mythology, Njörðr was offered in marriage to the ice giant Skadi as restitution for slaying her father. While Njörðr cherished the hustle and bustle of the fertile seaport, Skadi preferred the dead stillness of the dark northern landscape. Concessions were made so that they might spend equal time at the place of their choosing. This is a reminder that opposites, such as the warmth of summer sun and the icecaps of winter, can exist simultaneously within you. Compromise is needed in order to reestablish the balance between your emotional wealth and overall well-being.

When the sea turns choppy, the mast is frosted, and your boat is rocking and about to capsize or sink, Njörðr reminds you that you are neglecting your personal needs. It's time to stop focusing on other ships and chip the ice off your unfulfilled desires. Njörðr and Skadi realized that their differences were great and eventually they separated. In order to refill your emotional cauldron, you may need to sever emotional ties with certain people, places, or things.

WEST

The appearance of Njörðr as a playful west wind signifies that universal secrets of prosperity are bubbling below the surface and will soon be revealed. This widely venerated Norse god was shrouded in mystery. As the icecaps melt, a clear path will be revealed. Infuse your life with magic and discover a world of prosperity that lies beyond the horizon.

If Njörðr raises the sea and waves smack sideways into your ship, you must clear all obstacles from your path. Use discretion before moving forward, so as to not injure yourself or others. Icebergs loom deep beneath the water's surface; some secrets should be cherished and kept hidden. Gossip is capable of sinking any ship. Achieving prosperity requires diligence and hard work, as well as charting a new course of action.

NORTH

The appearance of Njörðr as a favorable north wind indicates that you are now ready to move beyond your current vision. Further your education and explore opportunities that cross your path. Alternate dimensions of reality are accessible through magic and faith.

According to legend, a war occurred between two sects of the Norse gods, the combative Aesir and the magical Vanir. After 100 years of conflict, neither side claimed victory. A truce was made and peace was restored. Similarly, a conflict requires a truce to prevent further damage to your garden. Graciously offer peace to a problematic situation in your life, so that the fertile earth can provide you with a bountiful harvest, the root of prosperity.

If Njörðr shipwrecks your plans, pinpoint the area where your actions are out of alignment with the good of the community. Ask Njörðr for protection as you plant your sacred seeds of prosperity and replenish your fields.

OYÁ (YORUBA)

Transformation

When you need power to cut through delusion and stagnation, call for Oyá. Women in business can summon her strength to help them succeed in the marketplace.

Oyá is a powerful wind goddess and a harbinger of change. She is an indigenous old-world *orisha* from Nigeria who, when called, will direct your spiritual ascension. *Orishas* are a manifestation of the divine spirit in African and Latin-American culture. From an indigenous perspective, *orishas* are seen as angelic emanations of one source, a self-existent being responsible for all of creation, manifestations, and destruction.[1] *Orishas* are angels, divine messengers from heaven, who have existed on record for over 12,000 years.[2]

Cultural expressions of Oyá extend beyond West African borders to Brazil, where she is known as Yansan. As a guardian of commerce, Oyá keeps a watchful eye on all activities occurring in the marketplace. Those who heed her message will see their struggling business rise from the ashes and transform into a prosperous enterprise. Her name means *she tore*, and if a business lacks integrity, Oyá rushes in and slices it up into shreds with her sword, ensuring that justice is served.

Oyá's husband, Shango, often accompanies her as a thunderous raging storm god. The combination of her sword and his fire purifies everything in their path, as they use hurricanes and cyclones to clear the way for divine intercession. Legend states, "What Oyá destroys, you no longer need."

Often disguised as a water buffalo, this goddess is a fierce protector of women, capable of violent outbursts whenever a wrong needs to be made right. Yet despite her fiery side, Oyá has a nurturing side, and is also known as a mother of nine, with her offspring representing the tributaries of the Niger River in Africa. When summoned by prayer, Oyá empowers mistreated women and engenders feminine leadership.

Whenever this passionate wind goddess appears, it is a fortuitous omen signifying that you are about to undergo a powerful spiritual transformation. Call to her when your life requires clarity and you need to cut through resistances and blocks.

EAST

When Oyá arrives as a tempestuous eastern wind, a rapid transformation of your belief system is imminent. Your ideas, plans, and memories may be scattered far and wide by the force of her raging storm. However, once this upheaval subsides, stillness will settle in. This is a time to be patient and watchful as vistas of exciting new possibilities are projected onto the screen of your mind.

Resisting change is a fruitless endeavor when Oyá appears as a headstrong wind. Surrendering and allowing Oyá to "clear the air" of old habits and rigid forms that stand in the way of progress will reveal new possibilities.

SOUTH

Without the invigorating breath of wind, stagnation sets in and death is sure to follow. Oyá appears as a purifying rainstorm to saturate and replenish your arid emotional landscape. She has arrived to assist your journey into your divine inner self. Offer her some homemade chocolate pudding as an expression of gratitude.

As a mother who has experienced the loss of a child, she understands that while you cannot always protect your children from the storm, your love can provide a safe haven. Call upon Oyá to guide you to a place of serenity so that you can nurture yourself or a loved one.

Are you stuck in an unhealthy situation or relationship? If Oyá arrives from the south, prepare yourself. Shango is never far away, and together they will ignite your inner fire. Oyá is here to protect you in a loving manner as she nudges you toward a place of calm and security.

WEST

A change of season is in the air when Oyá blows in from the western quadrant. As a gatekeeper of life, Oyá can guide you through transitions at home, business, or within your multidimensional self. Oyá can open doors and reveal new vistas. If you are experiencing a loss, keep in mind that the cycle you are presently experiencing is quickly waning. The fruits of your harvest will become evident after the next growing season.

If you are unwilling to clear your fields of negative thoughts and feelings, an adverse Oyá arrives on the scene. She manifests as a violent rainstorm to wash away all obstacles standing before you, so that you can embark upon a new journey with confidence and enthusiasm.

NORTH

Inner transformations unfold at a subconscious level before they become apparent. The presence of Oyá as a helping wind in the northern quadrant suggests that you may be on the cusp of a new cycle, and on the verge of great change. Oyá is preparing you to make a leap from your current state into the unknown. Even though your coordinates may not give a clear indication of your present condition, you can be sure that Oyá is aligning you with your magnetic north.

An intractable weather pattern may indicate deep spiritual forces are at work. Every change has a tipping point, where old forms and ideas are cast aside as a new, higher state of consciousness rises to the surface. Be patient and know that all is well; feeling unstable is part of this transformational process. Beckon Oyá to help you prepare for an initiation ritual.

SHU (ANCIENT EGYPTIAN)

Separation

Petition the calming winds of Shu to create more space in your life,
or to see more clearly into the gray area of life.

Egypt's history is mysterious, long, and rich as the black silt lining the banks of the north-flowing Nile River. Ancient Egyptian history is divided into three periods of civilization: the Old Kingdom (about 2,700–2,200 BCE), the Middle Kingdom (2,050–1,800 BCE), and the New Kingdom (about 1,550–1,100 BCE). Insight into ancient Egypt's cosmogony is gleaned from the sacred Pyramid Texts found at Heliopolis, dating back to the Old Kingdom, which included cosmogony expression, rituals, and incantations; the Coffin Texts, detailing maps to the realm of the afterlife; and the Wisdom Texts, outlining social norms passed from father to son.[1]

According to ancient Egyptian legend, Shu and Tefnut are the set of twins created by the god Atum, whose breath stirred life from the chaotic primordial waters. These twin gods and their offspring formed the Ennead of Heliopolis, the nine primary deities of Ancient Egypt. Shu and Tefnut's offspring were Geb (earth) and Nut (sky), who then gave birth to Osiris, Isis, Set, Nephthys, and Horus.[2] Shu's separation of the intertwined lovers Geb and Nut created the world of duality and form.

Shu is the ancient Egyptian god of the wind, the atmosphere, and the space between the heavens and the earth. He personifies air, and his name means "emptiness" or "he who rises up." Shu is characterized as a man with a lion's head, and carries the *ankh*, the symbol of life. The Coffin Texts tell us Shu influenced life on earth and protected the sun, while Tefnut ruled the upper domains of truth and justice.[3]

Throughout the ages, Egyptian myths shared common themes of fertility, rebirth, death, and resurrection. However, Shu's responsibilities and position in society morphed throughout the ages to suit the divine power and authority needed by each ruling king.

When Shu appears, there is a transformation of space taking place in your life. Beware of black-and-white thinking. A blind spot may be revealed, calling for a closer examination of a specific area in your life.

EAST

When Shu arrives from the east, you may feel inundated by chaos. Ideas may be diluted or get washed away. The annual flooding of the Nile created optimum conditions for agriculture in the northeast quadrant of Africa. Too much water could destroy villages, and during periods of drought there was very little to harvest. Order follows chaos. Once the water recedes, your thoughts and ideas will become fertile ground and the seeds you plant will sprout and grow quickly.

Divine order is determined by God's will. If you are not in harmony with Shu, projects may wither or die. Outmoded or rough ridges of beliefs may be swept away or buried below the silt. For balance, call upon Tefnut to whet your ideas with truth and justice before trying to move forward.

SOUTH

The Nile flows from south to north, and when Shu blows in from the south, buried emotions may wash up and inundate you. Upon close examination of your needs and desires, you may discover an unlikely source for your disharmony and malcontent. A job, relationship, or idea that appeared to be a polished gem may be pitted with scars caused by past emotional turmoil.

When the wind blows, dirt settles in these cracks, exposing and releasing raw emotional pain. This is a good time to ask,

"What changes do I need to make in my life in order to reestablish space and order?"

Shu accompanied his brother Ra (the sun) to the underworld each day, to protect him. When contrary winds blow your boat off course, and your own demons appear, call upon Shu's lion force for protection. Heavy energy only sticks when you have an affinity with its emotional origin.

WEST

Shu is often depicted as sitting in a chair and wearing one to four feathers on his head. Shu's duty is to maintain a separation between the sky and the earth. He represents a balance of earthly pursuits and spiritual aspirations. Shu is a preserving wind that can help restore balance in your life.

You have been holding up the sky too long, and it is time to release your burdens. When Shu arrives in the contrary position, it is time to pause and take responsibility for your health and well-being. Pay special attention to the cues of your body. Stress of any kind indicates that you are in need of physical, emotional, and/or mental healing. Take the time to rest, heal, and rejuvenate. Allow events to unfold in a natural, rhythmic manner.

NORTH

When Shu arrives as a bitterly cold north wind, the foundation of your faith and spiritual principles is being called into question. Allow yourself to connect with the winds of spirit, and trust your own inner wisdom when determining what is appropriate for you.

Shu's pervasive cold sweep may leave behind what appears to be a pile of rubble; but once this wind subsides, you will find many sparkling precious jewels awaiting you. Your faith in nature will be restored as you move forward in the loving embrace of the rivers and trees.

SILA INNUA (INUIT)
Wisdom

*Breathe in the winds of Sila Innua when you seek the
guidance and clarity of seeing with closed eyes.*[1]

For the Netsilk Inuit (Netsilingmiut) who live in Canada's
Nunatsiavut Territory, Sila Innua is the indweller of air (spirit). The
Netsilk Inuit occupy the land north of Quebec, in Newfoundland
and Labrador. The name Nunatsiavut means "our beautiful land,"
and as with everything else in the Netsilk Inuit cosmos, it has a
soul of its own.

During the long dark winters, the Netsilk Inuit travel by dog-
sled, while during the extended light of summer, they journey by
foot and kayak. Navigating across hundreds of miles is challenging, and life is dependent upon successfully locating and catching
salmon, seals, and caribou.[2] Blinding blizzards are part of everyday life on the lonely tundra; their world is shrouded in darkness for eight months of the year, and blanketed with fog during
the summer. The consistent prevailing winds provide a natural
compass for these indigenous hunters who travel long distances
in search of food.

The Inuit "evolved practices that allowed them to negotiate a
vast terrain that seems featureless to most Western eyes."[3] Knud
Rasmussen reported after his northern America expedition (1921
to 1924) that the Inuit had detailed spatial memory of their landscape.[4] When provided with writing implements (which they had
never used before), they were quickly able to outline the shape of
their country and add intricate details of the islands, peninsulas,
bays, and lakes.[5]

Survival of the elements required ingenuity, an understanding of the elements, and a deep spiritual reverence for life, merriment, and song. Long, harsh winters sparked the development of the art of storytelling. A multitude of myths and legends remain part of a culture whose borders extend from the southern tip of Siberia and across the Barren Strait into Greenland, northern Canada, and Alaska. The energy of Sila Innua is a common theme throughout these stories. This venerated wind is generally regarded as a formless, invisible wind energy possessing a plethora of special powers and attributes. Sila Innua is regarded as the soul of all objects, people, and animals as it follows them from one life into the next. Cooperating with this indwelling spirit of wind and breath is essential for survival.

To these sea hunters, every animate and inanimate component of the universe is permeated with the energy of Sila Innua. They believe their beautifully crafted weapons will encourage the spirits of animals to sacrifice their lives willingly. One myth refers to Sedna (another manifestation of Sila Innua), the sea mother who controls the elements of nature and responds with violent storms if traditional behavior is broken. The Angakkuts (shamans) are wary of losing favor with Sedna and make regular spirit flights to appease her, lest she threaten their livelihood.

If Sila Innua appears in your life, you are being called to tap into your intrinsic divine wisdom.

EAST

If Sila Innua appears in the east, it is time to pause, reflect, and think before taking action. The Inuit observe wind patterns and read the ripples in the snow before choosing their course of action. A different question may elicit many responses; sometimes nonaction is the appropriate stance. The Inuit believe that every word is imbued with a specific energy and meaning. If you are being buffeted by a cold arctic wind, consider "holding your tongue" until Sila Innua changes course.

Sila Innua may arrive as a side wind to remind you of the importance of selecting a name. Be conscientious when selecting a name for a new business or child, as the name will alter the outcome. One name, tuk'Artorwik ("the place where one tramps"), is next to the tribe's favorite winter fishing spot. Choose your words carefully, as they project a mental image to others.

SOUTH

If Sila Innua manifests in the southern quadrant, you are being advised to trust your intuitive guidance system. Rely on your sense of smell, as scent can evoke strong emotional information that can help you discern what food is best for you and how to select an appropriate romantic partner. Immerse yourself in your sensuous surroundings, as they offer signs that will lead you to your intended destination.

If Sila Innua shrouds your path with fog, it is easy to lose track and get off course. If your fight-or-flight response is engaged, it is time to pause and listen to the sea mother Sedna, who will show you how to reset your sails and get back on course.

WEST

When Sila Innua walks through the western door of your life, embrace the darkness as you look forward to sharing the light of dawn with friends and family. This is a time to spend with others by sharing stories, singing, crafting, playing games, walking in nature, or cooking.

If Sila Innua arrives as a cold wayward west wind, be content as you wait. Slowly wake up, get energized, and emerge from darkness. Get creative and reward yourself by revitalizing your living space with a beautiful makeover.

NORTH

When it's time to go inward and withdraw from the outer world, Sila Innua will blow in from the north. *Introspection, tranquility,* and *solitude* are the operative words here. The Inuit call this time *inutuaq*: choosing to walk with only your thoughts, in order to engender respect, wonder, and gratitude.

If your natural rhythm is out of sync, the north wind Kinak will blow with unusual force. This is a time to withdraw from the outer world. Focus on your inner self and reconnect with the raw nature of your own life. Turn off all your electronic devices and surrender, until you feel the wind reconnect you with the larger whole.

STRIBOG (SLAVIC)
Dispersal

*Call on Stribog when you need to disseminate information,
increase your wealth, or expand your awareness and receive
consensus for an idea or project.*

Slavs have occupied the most western part of Eastern Europe
since before the fifth century AD. The linguistic root is *slovo*,
meaning people who speak the same language or understand each
other. For centuries, the organizing principles of their faith and
shamanic rituals were kept hidden behind a veil of secrecy from
those who spoke in a different tongue.

The Slavs' three-world cosmology centered on a world tree.
This system was composed of seven primary deities that included
Stribog. In Slavic cosmogony, when Rod (creator god) broke free
from the cosmic egg, all the elements of nature, including the wind
from his breath, were pulled from his body. Stribog is the intermediary ancestor of wind who delivers (gives voice to) the prayers
and invocations of the people to their creator.

Stribog is also grandfather of the eight directional winds.
While he is often portrayed as Old Man Winter, he is also connected to the invigorating fresh air of spring. The roots of his
name are *stri* (to spread) and *bog* (God). Stribog is best known as
the disperser of wealth and spirit. The Slavs were pragmatic people
who intimately understood that living harmoniously with nature
required an understanding of the harsh winter winds, as well as
the cool summer breezes. Although the winds are severe and bitterly cold as they blow across the rivers and steppes, Slavic myths
still viewed Stribog as the deliverer of good fortune.

To this day, wind whisperers remain scattered throughout
the Ukraine, and they continue to use wind to cast spells and
send healing charms. The existence of these peasant shamans

is a testament to the enduring nature of these earth traditions. Ancient rock altars built to worship the gods have survived thousands of years of political and religious oppression.

Stribog arrives as a cool passionate breeze to remind you that every season is part of a larger life cycle. It is time to restore peace, rhythm, and order to your faith.

EAST

If Stribog soars in on the back of his eagle as an easterly spring wind, it means seeds of creation are being pollinated. New thoughts and ideas are abundant. Remember to ask, "Is now the time to act, or should I set my intentions to prayer for manifestation?" In either scenario, ask Stribog to answer your prayers. Patience is a deliberate action set forth by the mind. Once you decide to act, know that Stribog will blow fortune your way.

Stribog may arrive as a discordant chill, bearing unfavorable conditions, but remember that great intellectual discoveries are often uncovered due to necessity. If the cupboards are bare, and the house is cold, use your divine imagination to usher in the sun's warmth.

SOUTH

When Stribog appears as a southern wind, the timing is right to pollinate your emotional seeds. Inhale the rejuvenating cool air of humility into your rich emotional landscape. Use common sense when it comes to sadness and melancholy, as these are essential aspects of your soul's existence. Become the active observer and discover the gift you deserve. Offer up your gratitude to Stribog and share your tears of sadness with all of creation.

If Stribog clashes with your plans, it is time for deep introspection. Examine the areas where you are a slave to your feelings. Are you leaving a trail of emotional baggage wherever you roam? Ask Stribog to help you find peace and calm. In order to receive the exhilarating breath of unconditional love, you must first heal your emotional wounds, and then surrender to a higher power.

WEST

When Stribog, the disperser of wealth, arrives in the west, it is a sign that your prayers have been heard and answered. Smile and enjoy the fruits of your labor. An abundant harvest is intended to provide sustenance for the long winter ahead. However, be mindful of how you expend your energy. A wise person who is in sync with nature can enjoy a bountiful harvest while conserving valuable resources.

If Stribog blows a strong headwind into your sails, it's time to seek out and eliminate areas of resistance. Being prepared is essential. Ask yourself, "Have I left valuable resources rotting in the field?" Get your affairs in order and prepare for restrictions that will accompany the long nights ahead.

NORTH

Good fortune has arrived; your lucky star is here. The Slavs were pragmatic and grateful to be alive, regardless of external conditions. Prayers are a request, while meditation provides insight. Stribog reminds you it is necessary to give and receive every day. Acknowledge Stribog's energetic breath that greets you every morning when you wake up. Be grateful for the little things in life, such as the food you eat, the convenient parking space that suddenly appeared, and the sun that shines upon your face.

When Stribog blows in as a fierce cold north wind, it is time to get grounded and establish a practical working relationship with your creator. Peace can be elusive when you take more than you give. When Old Man Winter comes knocking at your door, it is time to reconnect with your tribe and volunteer your services in a loving manner. It may be time to renew your altar. Make your faith a dynamic spiritual expression that enriches both your soul and the community in which you live.

TĀWHIRIMĀTEA
(NEW ZEALAND)
Tempest

Summon this powerful wind when you seek impetus and motivation for change, or when your family or community needs protection.

About 50 generations ago (3,500 years), ancestors of the Māori left Polynesia and sailed eastward to populate the isolated Chatham Islands.[1] Since that time, native New Zealanders have protected their sacred place of belonging, "the land of the long white cloud." As guardians of their land, the Māori protect tradition, home, and family, while embracing adversity. *Kapa haka* is a dance used by Māori warriors to intimidate intruders. Each rhythmic dance move builds upon the next, and is anchored in the principle of oneness with the earth. Connection with the Earth Mother is the sacred heartbeat of every story, song, dance, dream, and decision.

Aggression and discord are primary themes in Māori cosmogony. In the beginning, darkness prevailed throughout the universe. Papatūānuku (Papa, the Earth Mother) and Ranginui (Rangi, the sky father) entwined in a passionate, loving embrace, creating only male offspring. As one might expect, frustration mounted as 70 gods competed for the power that lay wedged in the darkness. Dissension grew. While some progeny wanted to separate their parents, a few, including Tāwhirimātea, did not. After many unsuccessful attempts to free themselves, Tāne Mahuta (Tane, god of the forest and trees) planted himself firmly against Papa, and pushed Rangi into the heavens, bringing light and consciousness to our planet. He breathed the sacred breath (Ha) into the nostrils of the first woman—Hineahuone—and as he did so, he said, *"Tihei mauri ora!"* (Behold, there is life!)

Stricken by grief, Tāwhirimātea sided with his heavenly father, and together they plotted revenge on his brothers. Carrying the winds of each direction, his vengeful rage caused destruction across the planet. During his tantrum, he uprooted forests and disfigured the landscape, which gave rise to the New Zealand Alps. Then he erupted the volcanoes, which heated up the ocean and created the rocky island landscape. Out of fear, some life-forms fled to sea for safety, while reptiles settled inland. This led to the notion of "original separation." One of his brothers, Tūmatauenga (Tū), withstood his wrath and silenced him. This brave act led to the birth of civilization and the emergence of human consciousness.

Inherent in Māori cosmology is the idea that all life is subject to the power of storms, wind, and rain. Knowledge can be acquired through adversity, and wisdom is compounded from generation to generation.

When Tāwhirimātea charges headlong into your life, a power of sacred order (Tapu) is about to enter and "shake up" your daily life.

EAST

If you ask family members to recount the details of a story, you can be sure that many variations will emerge; the truth, however, usually lies somewhere between the lines. Māori legend states that New Zealand was settled by the sailors of a fleet of seven large canoes (*waka*) containing women, livestock, and basic supplies. In the 1950s, radiocarbon dating disproved this myth, yet many still cling to the original story. If Tāwhirimātea appears in the east, your prevailing stories and beliefs are going against the wind, and will be uprooted.

It is time to surrender long-held ideas; your landscape is about to be radically transformed by the force of this storm. In its wake, a new cycle will emerge. Proceed cautiously, and consider how your new choices will impact future generations.

If fear rages into your life, ask yourself, "What is the root of my suffering?" An illusion of separation appears when you feel superior, less than, or different from another. The Māori believe that all humans share a similar ancestry, and that invisible strands of light connect everything in the universe.

SOUTH

When Tāwhirimātea storms in, it's time to move out of your comfort zone. Despite the love of Rangi and Papa, darkness prevailed due to their intimate coupling. Light was needed for humanity to grow and flourish. Often pain and resistance are gifts that lead to the greatest growth. Embrace the wrath of Tāwhirimātea. Ask for the willingness to draw upon your life experiences, so you can find compassion and understand your complex emotions.

As Tāwhirimātea circled the skies, his tantrum caused the very thing he was avoiding—the feeling of separation. Similarly, your emotional windstorm is wreaking havoc upon your family and community. It is time to consider the negative effects of your selfish behavior on others. An apology is meaningless without a change in behavior. Extended grief can produce ill effects and reap destruction in your life.

WEST

When Tāwhirimātea comes in with enormous force from the west, pay close attention to any aromas that may accompany him. Scent is key to partner selection, meal preparation, and choosing a home. Death has a distinctive smell that permeates the atmosphere whenever a person exhales his or her last breath.

Tāwhirimātea has arrived to teach you that certainty is possible, even in the midst of unpredictable weather patterns. Every fall, a storm hits the South Island with a cold blast and two claps of thunder, before it annihilates the sea village. This is a reminder that destruction is a natural aspect of life.

If Tāwhirimātea swamps your *waka*, it is time to see where you have become imbalanced. Once we stop taking, we learn about giving and receiving. In order to guarantee regeneration in your life, practice tossing your first fish back into the waters of plenty.

NORTH

When Tāwhirimātea blows in from the north, he energizes your fearless imagination. Endings are like spiritual threads in a vivid tapestry, woven together to represent your multilayered world. Artistic expression is the embodiment of spirit. Life has become routine and the time has come to fan the flames of your divine creativity.

When Tāwhirimātea arrives as a fierce warrior wind, it is time to rest and rejuvenate. Like children wedged between their parents, ideas cannot germinate in a dark, limited, suffocating space. If you want your plans to grow and flourish, you must provide a healthy, supportive, nutrient-rich, spiritual environment.

TȞATÉ (LAKOTA SIOUX)
Messenger

Sing a sacred song to this wind when you seek spiritual guidance
and desire to have a closer connection with the natural world.

Reverence for all life is at the core of Lakota tradition. The stories are kept alive in their sun dances, medicine ceremonies, and community customs. Wind makes its presence known as it moves through space and time. Knowledge is accumulated as you live through many winters and offer your services to the community. It is important that you find serenity in nature and in the Inipi (lodge). In the Lakota tradition, messages from spirit are personal, sacred, and not freely shared, even among medicine people.

Lakota legend says that in the beginning, Skan was the unmoving, energizing force of the universe. To provide impetus to move his creations throughout time and space, he created Tȟaté as his faithful messenger. Tȟaté is the messenger of Wakan Tanka (creator, Great Mystery). "The wind is considered the breath of the creator, the breath of the mystery. That breath united all living creatures on earth. The wind is considered as essential as water and light and the cosmos."[1] To engage with the spirit of this invisible wind, your senses must be highly attuned.

Winds created the space and time division of the Lakota cosmology, the four parts of the day, the quarters of the moon, and the four moon times (seasons) of the year. Time is a relative concept. There are four cycles of time moving in a circular motion: daytime, nighttime, moon time, and year time. The first three times circle above the world and in the regions of the underworld, but the year time circulates around the world.[2] This ordered universe creates form and stability, fluidity, and growth.

Life begins in the lodge, which represents a microcosm of the world. The Inipi ceremony is ordered, and while inside the darkened womb, one loses track of all time and space. Life is based on cause and effect, and as a new god/goddess, person, or element is brought into the circle, the dynamic relationship between everything shifts, creating a new plateau for change. Change is carried upon the wind.

Before humans inhabited planet Earth, Tȟaté lived in the Inipi with his four sons, the directional winds: Eya (west), Yata (north), Yanpa (east), and Okaga (south). In one Sioux myth, a dishonest woman is brought into the lodge (*tipi*). She kills three of the four brothers when they try to woo her with their magic. Okaga, the youngest brother, evades her charm, claims his power, and erects a second *tipi*.[3] Using his own magical powers, he resurrects his dead brothers. We can understand this as a message that oppositional forces can disrupt order, resulting in growth and evolution.

In Lakota cosmology there is an understanding that disruption and discomfort are sacred elements that can facilitate personal growth and change. The sons of Tȟaté blow in from the four directions to offer divine guidance and help you navigate safely through life.

EAST

A new day is dawning when Tȟaté sends Yanpa, the east wind, to greet you. If your senses are properly attuned, you will receive a clear, powerful vision. In the same manner that the sun energizes and illuminates the sky, complex ideas will become easy for you to comprehend. Work with this wind to highlight the essential and avoid diversion and distraction. Take time to organize and devise plans in silence. Solitude and secrecy are called for, so keep your ideas to yourself.

If you are moving too quickly and are out of sync with nature, Tȟaté may manifest as quarrels, illness, or obstacles blocking your path. If you are sick or lack motivation, call on Tȟaté for clarity and direction.

SOUTH

Tȟaté blows in as a southern wind to upset your emotional balance, so you can learn and appreciate the value of cooperation. Call upon the sacred wind to bring forth the elements of change. It is imperative to harmonize your emotions, which may require a shift in your current living conditions or work situation. Cooperation is the key to balance.

Also possible is the arrival of the whirlwind, Yum, Tȟaté's faithful companion. This guarantees lighthearted messages of fun, children, laughter, luck, and love.

Don't get discouraged if the south wind arrives as Iktomi (trickster), a master of malcontent. Once you interpret the message, truth will be revealed, illusions will vanish, and emotional growth will begin.

WEST

It is time to enter the lodge, sit peacefully, and wait. Prayer and meditation are calming forces of nature. Once the answers are clear, call upon Tȟaté to help you move forward in a joyous celebration.

Pay close attention, as Tȟaté may come disguised as a loud clap of thunder, a denizen of the forest, or an eagle. Once you receive the message, clear the way by removing the debris from your home, heart, and mind. It's time for a feast. Prepare a meal and invite supportive friends and family to a "giveaway ceremony." Open your heart and extend genuine blessings to the world at large.

Pain in specific areas of your body indicates where you are resisting the wind. Stiff joints may be signs of inflexibility. Back problems are signals of not feeling supported, and a stiff neck may indicate an unwillingness to see things as they truly are. Ask Tȟaté for divine guidance, as discomfort can guide healing.

NORTH

When Tȟaté blows in from the north, it is time to center your soul and receive healing via a purification ceremony. A long cycle of grief may be coming to an end. If you are harboring thoughts that require clearing, or feel a need to forgive others, seek solitude and ask Tȟaté for guidance. It is time to heal any spiritual scars that remain as barriers to personal growth. Riches are bestowed and your spirit is strengthened when you tend to the needs of your soul.

If Tȟaté arrives as a bitter cold wind, you are reminded to purify your body, mind, and emotions. Are you selfish and unwilling to change? The grounds before you have frosted over and everything green may wither and die. Tȟaté's message may arrive as a phantom in the night and disrupt your peace. Harmony needs to be restored before the frozen earth can soften and reveal the path that leads to spiritual healing. Forgiveness will cleanse and reenergize your spirit, emotions, thoughts, and actions.

VAYU (INDUS)
Strength

Hum the Tarā mantra; Hūm (Om) is the sound
of the wind as it blows with force when strength is needed.

In Indian mythology, Vayu is a supreme deity who rules the space between the sun and Earth. As a giver and taker of life, his role includes balancing light and dark energies. He is also known as a purifier, explorer, messenger of the gods, and leader of sacrifices.[1] As one of the strongest gods, Vayu is portrayed as a white man carrying a bow and arrows as he sits atop a deer. He is often seen accompanying Vishnu's golden chariot.

Vayu is attributed to severing the peak of Mount Meru, a sacred mountain in Indus cosmogony. In one tale, the omnipresent Vayu overhears two *gandharvas* (nature spirits) discussing the strength of Vasuki, the snake *deva* (god). According to their narrative, Vasuki originally created the world. He transformed himself into a rope that anchored the very first boat to a horn fish, which allowed the Lord to emerge from the stormy sea. Upon hearing this, Vayu became enraged and a battle with Vasuki ensued. Vasuki wrapped himself around Mount Meru three times, and Vayu blew his breath full force in an attempt to uncoil hm. As Vayu blew harder, the mountain swayed, and Vasuki tightened his grip. Mount Meru ordered them to cease their battle lest he tumble into the sea and put an end to civilization. Brahma appeased Vayu and Vasuki by praising their virtues. As Vasuki released his grip, the peak of Mount Meru sank into the sea.

An understanding of Vayu provides insights into the intrinsic nature of time, space, karma, life, and death.[2] Vayu is viewed as a formless, spiritual wind, a prevailing, dynamic force of nature that energizes all life but, when absent, invariably leads to stagnation and death.

EAST

The appearance of Vayu in the east signifies that now is the time to use the power and strength of your mind to undertake something new in your life.

Like Vasuki, ideas can be steadfast and stubborn. Thoughts are neither good nor bad; some are lighter, while others are denser. Vayu is asking you to become more aware of your thoughts and memories.

The time has arrived to stop comparing your gifts with those of others. Are you clinging to outmoded ideas? Patience is required and timing is of the utmost importance.

SOUTH

Vayu is a temperamental, stubborn wind known for his sudden outbursts. Progress is slow when we react from a place of resentment, pain, or anger. Use the power of Vayu to visualize your negative emotions gracefully exiting your body. Once Vayu relaxed and stopped resisting, an island of peace and harmony manifested.

If Vayu contradicts your peace stemming from an oppositional emotion, hold on, and sway with the breeze. Be observant and patient. When the time is right, respond accordingly.

WEST

Vayu can always be felt, but never seen. Likewise, our actions are often invisible to others and ourselves. Have faith in your strength. Tap into the powerful energy of Vayu before you embark upon a journey or commence a project. Be patient and you will be amply rewarded.

If Vayu is blowing against you, you may have to surrender, pause, and reenergize before moving on. It makes sense to work alongside community members during the harvest, for there is strength in numbers. Proceed with caution; Vayu is said to have fathered hundreds of offspring because of his impetuousness.

NORTH

The arrival of Vayu from the north signifies that an energetic interplay between static and dynamic winds is taking place within you. You are being challenged to look deeply into your inner core and discover your life's purpose as a spiritual being. Your actions, or lack thereof, will directly impact your fate and karma.

The northwest quadrant is where Vayu makes his home. He will blow into your face forcefully and incessantly until you learn how to connect with the formless invisible energy residing within. Thoughts, feelings, and actions are manifestations of latent creative energies. What are you expressing in your life today? What are you pouring into your divine matrix, the web of life?

VĒJA MĀTE (LATVIAN)

Nourishment

*Invoke the wind mother when
you need comfort and divine intervention.*

The nature-loving serfs who occupied the remote lands east of the Baltic Sea had little interest in outside world affairs, and kept their traditions underground for generations. *Dzīvesziņa* (life knowledge), passed on in the form of *dainas* (folklore), provided transgenerational continuity and insight into the serfs' sacred relationship with nature. *Dainas* were preserved though song. Because the meter and tone does not permit the substitution of words and phrases, their lyrics have remained intact throughout the centuries.[1]

While the early agricultural religion of the Balts had its roots in the mystical contemplative traditions of India, Latvians exercised a more practical and interactive approach to prayer through song. Testaments of their strong faith live on in the archives of over 500,000 songs (*dainas*).[2]

Up until the late 14th century AD, the mother god religion flourished in the swampy forests. The triad of *dievs* (goddesses) comprised the Saule (Dual-Sun), Māra (Earth), and Laime (Fortune). The sun goddess was responsible for two suns, one that rose daily and one in the netherworld. Māra, the great Earth Mother, had dominion over matter; she was the giver, preserver, and taker of life. The goddess Laime was lady luck and fortune. While the parameters of one's fortune were set at birth, many *dainas* spoke of free will and responsibility: "each the forger of his luck, don't wait for Laime with your decorated mittens on, Laime as a grain for a blind chicken; misfortune comes without greeting, but calling fortune won't bring her."[3] Those born under the right star, who make responsible decisions and take appropriate action, are blessed with good luck.

One of the nutritive *dievs* is Vēja Māte, the mother wind. Wind brings rain, which nourishes the rye crops required to make bread. Agricultural celebrations marked significant events in time as the sun moved across the heavens. Rituals included the *vasaras saulgrieži* (summer solstice), *ziemas festivāls* (winter solstice), *lielā diena* (Easter/spring equinox), and the several autumn harvest festivals (fall equinox).[4] Many *dainas* reflect the importance of the mother goddesses, Veļu Māte (shade mother of death), Mežu Māte (forest mother), Darzamate (garden mother), Jurus Māte (sea mother), and Ūdens Māte (water mother), to name a few.[5]

When Vēja Māte evokes a wind-formed song, you are reminded that Mother Earth will take care of all your needs. It is time to "harness your winds, as a horse to a yoke,"[6] and sing your praises to the goddess.

EAST

Optimism lies at the core of Latvian nature worship. The wind mother offers an endless supply of goodness, which is available to those who pay homage to nature. Everything is possible when you take responsibility for your actions. Climb a mountain and sing your praises for the gifts she has bestowed upon you.

Are you prone to telling disruptive stories or songs? Vēja Māte encourages you to focus your attention on the abundant gifts of nature, and to be grateful for the air you breathe. If luck continues to pass you by, Vēja Māte reminds you to forge ahead confidently, because luck will eventually find you. Beware of envy, mistrust, and jealousy.

SOUTH

Vēja Māte might arrive as a windy storm, causing distant memories to rise to the surface of your consciousness. She may also appear as a rainy-day love song and stir your emotions. Healing can be triggered by broken contracts, feuds, divorce, death, or betrayals. The sun goddess often arrived in tandem with the wind mother to create dissension; a certain feud myth describes a dispute at a wedding; this dramatic tale is designed to encourage resolution and summon a rebirth.[7] True nourishment comes from soaking in the summery salted waters of the bay and feeling connected with the dynamic web of life. Within this framework reside the good, the bad, the ugly, and the beautiful. True compassion arises when all of nature's manifestations are understood and accepted.

The Latvian people regard frogs and snakes as sacred creatures. If Vēja Māte blows one onto your path, it's time to shed tears of gratitude. The warm wind brings cleansing rains of transformation. This is an ideal time to be creative, and to restore peace and harmony in your life.

WEST

As she heads westward toward the sea, Vēja Māte howls with the force of a gale. She brings a powerful, loving message reminding you to plan carefully before taking action. Prior to the sun setting on the present growing season, be sure to till the soil and prepare for the next cycle. Just as the white of an egg blends perfectly with the yolk, your well-planned efforts will ensure that you harvest a bountiful crop next year.

If an early frost suddenly appears and disrupts your plans, accept its presence and surrender to the process. Remain cheerful as the cold winds connect you with the cyclical rhythm of nature. Shine from within; release the warmth and beauty of your inner sun.

Death stalks you in the west, breaking loose old patterns. The Balts placed women and men horizontally in a single grave. They were buried with their own tools as an everlasting reminder that balance and harmony are found in asymmetrical relationships.[8] If the wind feels stagnant and cold, Vēja Māte is asking you to respect and honor your sacred masculine and feminine aspects.

NORTH

Vēja Māte is the emanating force that stimulates and nurtures your creativity. As temperatures plunge into the single digits, you are reminded that it is time to gather around the fire with friends to craft and share stories. In the matriarchal order of the Balts, men and women participated in separate activities. This was a conscious and visible act of cooperation in service to the greater whole. These groups of men and women intersected with the larger cycle of nature, creating interdependence and perfect synergy.

Vēja Māte blows in as a cold, biting wind to let you know that you are not alone. Secure a piece of amber as a reminder that the nurturing, loving warmth of mother sun will soon return. The mother only creates ornate matter that has a purpose, so be sure to cherish it. Everything is born, grows, and dies in perfect order. A divine nourishing wind can always be found in the soil of a fallow field.

WAYRAMAMA (PERUVIAN)
Right Relationship

*Kiss the air as you gracefully call
upon this wind to help restore harmony.*

The Quechua-speaking Indians of Peru originally lived in the remote Andean highlands, where the air is rarefied. Families lived in single-room, dirt-floor mud huts. Winters were harsh above the tree line; alpaca dung was used to heat the central fire. The nomadic Alpaca herders and steppe farmers developed several hundred strains of potatoes and corn. Farming on the steep rocky hillside terraces was a strenuous activity that created strong, resilient communities.

The Q'ero were the keepers of the Vicuna, and the Weavers of the soft cloth that was the apparel of the Inka. Unlike the people in the cities below, who incorporated Catholicism into their daily ritual practices, they kept their oral wisdom tradition intact. In 1949, they descended by foot and traveled for three days to attend an annual celebration at the Sacred Mountain Ausangate (Apu Awsanqati), where they were welcomed by their fellow *paqos* (spiritual leaders). The Indians were recognized by the patterns woven into their ponchos and shawls.

To this day, a ritual prayer offering in the form of *kintus* is made with a packet of three cocoa leaves, as an expression of gratitude. These bundles represent the layered universe of indigenous way showers. The top leaf represents the Hanak Pacha, the home of the moon and the sun. Kay Pacha is the middle world, and the bottom leaf is Uku Pacha of the lower domains. Intentions are delivered to spirit via the breath of the wind.

"To kiss the air was in Peru the commonest and simplest sign of adoration to the collective divinities."[1] In nature, balance is maintained via geomancy, sacrifice, and prayers. For ancient

Peruvians, mountain and wind spirits were powerful benefactors who came to their aid when called. The Indians of Peru believed that the *apus* (mountain lords) manifested as earthquakes, throwing down rocks to block the path of advancing Spanish invaders.

Wayramama, the mother of the sky (envisioned as a great serpent that moves with a great wind), is one of several wind energies circulating throughout the Andes. "It is said that when she takes a bath, the sound of thunder is heard between the clouds, but no rain will fall."[2] Power is the capacity to transform energy by aligning with natural forces. The *apus* serve as intermediaries between *paqos* and the gods/goddesses of each domain.

These Peruvians have a deep respect for, and a harmonious relationship with, nature. They believe time and space are not linear concepts; they are based on a pattern of energy. The invisible energetic lines emanate from the Qorikancha, in Cuzco (the belly), and extend to sacred points throughout the Incan empire. The time/space intersections are called *ceques*. Sacred sites were built strategically along these energy lines. Sequences of mountains, rocks, outcroppings, caves, and stone forts have been built in accordance with astrological cycles. Hundreds of *haucas* (holy places) dot the landscape of the Tahuantinsuyu, which is composed of four *suyus* (geographical areas). Shamans believe that these *haucas* can manifest in many different forms of consciousness such as people, birds, and wind. Winds disseminated from these entities can be benevolent, disruptive, or deadly.

All living things are animated by the power of spirit. This concept is based on the sacred seed of reciprocity: today for me, tomorrow for you. All actions flow from this core principle of balance (*Ayni*), radiating outward from the heart, like the *ceque* lines found in the temple of the sun. *Ayni* ensures survival. Growing potatoes on shallow terraces stacked along steep mountain cliffs requires community effort. All selfless actions are complementary; today you receive, so tomorrow you must give back.

The appearance of Wayramama in your life means you must take direct action in order to restore balance in your life. Allow the supernatural forces of the wind to guide you.

EAST

When Wayramama appears in the east, she is ushering in a rebirth of thought. When the missionaries brought Christianity to Peru, some beliefs were complementary and easily integrated, while others, like original sin, were contrary to Incan beliefs and therefore rejected. Christian statues were only embraced as if they were alive with *kawsay* (life force energy). Now is the time to listen to and lead with your heart, look for the aliveness in all things, and allow your mind to shape your memories and dreams into a practical living reality.

Wayramama can be *mal viento*, creating confusion, chaos, and doubt. Like your Andean brothers and sisters, look to nature to provide you with the proper spiritual guidance.

SOUTH

When mother wind appears in the south, examine how you are expressing yourself and transmitting energy into the world around you. Are you giving and receiving in a balanced manner, or are you leaking energy? A reciprocal transfer of energy is necessary if a transaction is to be successful.

If the furious winds of the Wayramama appear, it is time to give close examination to your less desirable traits. Thievery, deceit, laziness, and incest create *hucha* (heavy energies) and discord. Now is the time to forgive yourself and others so that you may restore balance in your life.

WEST

If the wind currents of Wayramama appear in the west, a death of some kind is imminent. Death can take many forms: the ending of a job or relationship, a physical death, or the dissolution of an outmoded idea or behavior. Lighten your load, clear your energy, and make room for a transformation.

"According to Don Humberto's Sonqo from Colpa Kucho Q'eros, 'Machu Wayra' is the ancestral wind that comes from the Ukhu Pacha. It is a neutral wind but can manifest to help or harm depending on our relationship with our ancestors. This is why it's always a good idea to clear ancestral Hoochas and honor our ancestors."[3] Often, physical symptoms will appear in order to bring about a needed change. In Peru, shamans are recognized and chosen when they are struck by lightning. Are you answering the call in your life?

NORTH

Wayramama arrives in the north to remind you that *being* and *doing* must meld together as a single process. It is time to return to the source and fertilize your dreams. Take a hike to the top of a mountain where the stream originates, and offer a prayer of gratitude to the *huaca*.

When your dreams do not reflect your desires, Wayramama may be blowing in reverse. It is time to exercise the proper use of power. Exhale and release all of your doubts, fears, and disappointments into a blade of grass, and allow the Wayramama to carry them away.

YAPONCHA (HOPI)

Moderation

Ask Yaponcha to bring balance in every area of life.

Despite 2,000 years of obstacles such as war, famine, drought, floods, and the extinction of entire clans, the oral traditions of the Hopi remain intact today. Collectively, the Hopi comprise more than 150 older seed-gathering tribes including the Bear Clan (Hona-wungwa), the Strap Clan (Bia-quois-wungwa), the Blue Bird Clan (Chosh-wungwa), and the Spider Clan (Koking-wungwa).[1] Insight into their mysterious origins can be found in their songs, which offer continuity between the past and present. The Hopi god Yaponcha is the life-giving breath, a wind that makes his home in the crack of a rock at Sunset Crater.

According to legend, the Hopi ascended through a reed, passing through rock layers and mighty winds from the lower world. They emerged from a single hole of the darkened earth into an area known today as the Grand Canyon. Máasaw, the earth guardian, instructed them to wander, gather seeds, experience the land, and find a home imbued with spiritual harmony.[2] As these Uto-Aztecan speaking clans migrated, they created settlements throughout the southwest. Traces of their ancient footprint remain intact. They can be found in the black mesa area of northern Arizona, where remnants of their multiroom stone communities, petroglyphs, pottery chards, and baskets predate the eighth century AD. Order among the clans was maintained through Katsinas (Kachinas), stories, and ritual songs, which offer strict principles for living cooperatively in accordance with the Hopi tradition called *life way*. *Life way* refers to the beliefs, principles, practices, and daily rituals that enable them to live by corn grown with rain.[3]

In the hot, arid desert climate of northern Arizona, wind and rain are essential for survival. To understand the importance of Yaponcha within the context of Hopi lore, one must understand that growing corn was the predetermined lifeblood of their existence. Cooperating with the temperamental nature of the desert was critical for survival and resided in the heart of their everyday songs.

The inhabitants of the village were concerned that if Yaponcha blew too hard, their crops would not grow. Two "little fellows" were given the responsibility of talking with Yaponcha. They traveled for many days before reaching the mountain where he lived. Upon deliberation, they decided to seal the crack in the rock with a cornmeal mush. Within days of their victory over the wind, the air became dry and hot. Soon the villagers felt suffocated and realized moderation was the key to healthy crops and a thriving community. The "little fellows" were sent back to the crater, where they removed some of the cornmeal so the wind could be restored. Since that day, the wind has blown just enough to keep the people happy without destroying their crops. It is the responsibility of everyone in the community to do their part to maintain this harmony.

The arrival of Yaponcha signifies that moderation is necessary if you wish to attain spiritual balance in your life.

EAST

The gift of Yaponcha as a steady east wind may symbolize prosperity and fulfillment. You are being rewarded for your humble adherence to the traditions of your community. Nourishing rain falling upon your parched desert is the ultimate gift from the creator; your newly planted seeds will now germinate. Daily rituals, such as singing, will restore inspiration. Reciprocity is the key to living a balance life.

Whirling thoughts may be a sign that Yaponcha is blowing hard against your forward movement. Self-discipline is called for. Center yourself, become still like the eye of the storm, and ask what steps are required to move forward.

SOUTH

When Yaponcha arrives from the south, you are reminded that acceptance of self and others creates a state of emotional well-being. Individual differences should be respected, and you should moderate your temperament in such a way as to benefit the community. Self-restraint may be needed. Put your entire heart into a project so that others may benefit.

It is time to examine your morals and make sure your actions are aligned with your guiding principles. Are you exaggerating your own self-importance to gain power over others? Your victories may be short-lived like those of the "little fellows" in the Hopi story. They were proud of conquering the wind, and laughed all the way back to the village. Look beyond the pride of your achievements. Will your short-lived pleasure sustain the growth of your crops?

WEST

If Yaponcha appears as a west wind, you may be overindulging by gathering more seeds at the expense of others. In community it is important that everyone has enough to eat. Excessive eating and drinking is a strong wind that will leave your fields barren. It is time to make an offering to the Katsinas. Use the wisdom of your hands to create balance by crafting, cooking, or clearing the garden of debris and weeds. Offer a gift of kindness to a friend in need.

A shortness of breath or forgetting to breathe may indicate that the winds of Yaponcha are stalled. Stop and take a few deep breaths before proceeding.

NORTH

Your ability to make rain depends on the strength of your devotion. Yaponcha comes as a chilly north wind reminding you to sing, dance, laugh, and pray. Practice your devotion daily, year after year, at work, at home, in the fields, and during ceremony, to reinforce your success in growing corn (bringing your gifts to harvest). Be willing to discover the proper intensity of wind in your life, lest you become stagnant or so forceful that you extinguish the light of your dreams. Take an "artist date" in which you spend time in a museum, art gallery, or with your own creative pursuits. It is time to share your dreams and visions with everyone in your community.

Have the seeds you planted failed to grow? Yaponcha's swirl comes as a reminder to be grateful for the blessings in your life. Signs may be as subtle as a fallen feather, a light breeze, or an unexpected phone call. Instilling harmony into the community may require a personal sacrifice.

YEL ANA
(TURKISH; YÖRÜK)

Guidance

When the sands are shifting, invoke the wind mother to provide the patience necessary to wait out the brewing storm.

With its close proximity to Asia and Africa, Turkey was at the hub of ancient civilizations responsible for advancing agriculture and technology. The fertile landscape provided ideal conditions for humans to develop intimate relationships with forests, mountains, rivers, seas, and deserts. The wandering tribes (Yörük) who traveled throughout Anatolia were wind believers, offering sacrifices to the wind goddess Yel Ana.

Yel means *wind*, and *ana* (*ene*) means *mother.* Women were the caretakers of homes. They oversaw the survival of the community, and were responsible for conducting tribal rituals. As the feminine aspect of the wind, Yel Ana represents a mother's patience with her children, even when they misbehave. Women perfected the art of storytelling as a means to guide and teach their children. Their wisdom endured time as the basis for religious mythology. Stories about what happened when people lost favor with nature have been passed along for eons, including the story of the Great Flood as described in the Christian Bible.

Archaeological remains found in ancient sites like Çatalhöyük prove that goddess worship was a core element of old Turkish faith. Symbols found on statues, as well as rock art, illustrate that ancient goddesses were deemed responsible for creation, law, and order. They were also inventors of language, givers of wisdom, and bringers of order, rhythm, and truth.[1]

At the core of Turkish belief was a deep respect for nature and the mother goddess. Wind-slapped and dizzy with hunger, these people meandered slowly with their camels across the ever-changing landscape during their annual migration. For days, powerful dust-laden windstorms (*simoom*) would blow violently, constantly shifting the sand and obliterating most landmarks. During these storms, the desert herders relied on intuition to guide them safely to their destination.

The appearance of Yel Ana signifies that a *simoom* is blowing through your life. This is a time to pause, reflect, and be patient. Like the herders traveling through the desert, Yel Ana is asking you to bolster your faith and listen to your inner voice of wisdom before proceeding.

EAST

Ancestral nomads were keen observers of constellations and used the temperate night sky as their map to help them navigate safely through harsh, ever-changing landscapes. Yel Ana is beckoning you to observe your thoughts carefully; they will determine the quality and nature of your experiences as you journey through life. Like shifting sand in the wind, thoughts may mutate over time. Self-mastery requires patience, if you seek the truth during the inconstant phases of the moon.

If Yel Ana is pelting your backside with grains of sand, be on guard, because your mind may be playing tricks on you. Halt before proceeding, and ask, "Where am I out of sync? Am I hungry, angry, lonely, or tired?"

SOUTH

Yel Ana's appearance in the south indicates that you need to hunker down, stay put, keep your mouth closed, and listen. Relax and pamper yourself. Know that the entire community benefits and flourishes when every individual is safe and healthy.

Emotions can be like lone mugwort bushes in the desert, exposed to nature's harsh elements. Yel Ana's screeches can be heard above your cries when her composure turns bleak. Seeds may remain dormant while you survive the drought. Pain can be the patient fruit of the caper bush, slowly ripening and waiting for the wind to shift. Whenever the wind exposes your raw emotions, take time to heal, and remember that the pain shall pass with the shifting winds. Go to the mountains, where the earth goddess lives, and ask how to deal with your emotions in a creative manner. Invoke the earth to help you heal.

WEST

To the untrained eye, the desert is a homogeneous landscape with no distinguishable features. To a keen observer, however, there are subtle clues and signposts that lead to one's intended destination. Create your own sacred milestone as you tend to your harvest. You can create rock altars in the field as symbols of your gratitude. It is time to infuse sacredness into every aspect of your life, including your harvest.

The goddess Yel Ana asks you to organize, nurture, and protect the physical space inside your home. Like the nomads who created wind blocks with their tents, Yel Ana suggests that it is time to create a safe and secure environment, which is essential for your well-being, as well as that of your loved ones.

When a project feels like it is at a standstill, Yel Ana may feel like an unruly force of nature. However, everything always happens at the perfect time. Your diet, exercise, and habits have their own cycles, and the harsh wind blowing against your plans is a perfect message from nature. Sometimes doing nothing is the best way to surrender to the wind.

NORTH

Seeing clearly when Yel Ana blows in from the north requires you to trust in great, unseen powers. It is time to penetrate the deeper aspects of your inner self through ceremony and ritual. These components are necessary if you want to achieve balance and joy in yourself, your home, and your community. All joy stems from within and floats outward on the breath of the wind.

Yel Ana antagonism can create a barren or bruised landscape. This a time to pause, reflect, and determine whether you are manifesting your dreams, wishes, and aspirations. What is full must be emptied. Ask Yel Ana to enter your life and show you how to manifest peace, harmony, and happiness in your life.

YEONGDEUNG HALMANG
(TAMNA)
Balance

Beckon this wind goddess when you seek order and balance.
Summon her for rituals and a bountiful harvest.

Dawn breaks earliest across the fertile lands of northeast Asia, shedding light on a complex culture whose indigenous traditions have survived for eons, despite scant documentation and strict political deterrents. Yeongdeung Halmang, the child wind goddess, makes an appearance during the Chilmeoridang Yeongdeunggut. *Halmang* is a Jeju-dialect word meaning both "grandmother" and "goddess." The female deities are nearly always called *halmang* whether depicted as young, middle-aged, or elderly. The most common translation is *goddess*.[1] During her stay, villagers gather to pray for calm seas, a plentiful catch, and an abundant harvest.[2]

Jeju, an island of 18,000 gods, adds intrigue to the history of ancient Korea. While indigenous practices disappeared from the history books, *keun-gut* (great shamanic rituals) survived typhoons, incessant winds, wars, and drought. Jeju lies south of the Korean mainland, between China and Japan. The strategic military location of this peaceful community has made it a casualty of war throughout Korean history.

Myth states that Seolmundae Halmang is the divine creator giantess embodied by the omnipresent Mount Halla, who watches over Jeju, a mysterious land of volcanoes. At the beginning of the universe, the giantess created Mount Halla with a mere seven shovels of dirt. Some of the dirt escaped through her tattered skirt and formed secondary parasitic cones called *oerum*. Seolmundae Halmang accidentally fell into a cauldron of boiling soup, which her sons consumed by mistake. After discovering what they had done, they cried such bitter tears that their grief transformed them into rocks. These 380 *oreum* are the silent generals who help Grandmother (the giantess) watch over the island. Each spring, their tears revive multicolored azalea blossoms that blanket Mount Halla.[3]

Haenyeo are the independent, hardworking women of Jeju who make their living by manually harvesting fish from the ocean floor.[4] These women dive without breathing equipment, wearing lead weights as they descend into the sea to depths of 33 feet.[5] Farming the rocky earth offers many difficulties, including years of barren harvests, which can cause famine. Their community is bound together by a strong faith, which is expressed through their rituals.

During Yeongdeunggut, all activities such as fishing, moving, traveling, and household repairs are suspended. Community members prepare for the arrival of Yeongdeung Halmang by cleaning and cooking. The *haenyeo* adorn their homes and kitchens with offerings of specially prepared foods to ensure that the fishing winds will blow in their favor.[6] A "fickle cold" wind portends the grandmother's arrival. She stays for a fortnight, arriving on the first day of the second lunar month of the year.[7] An elaborate three-part ritual is performed in honor of her arrival; her visit determines the fate of the harvest. If she arrives as a strong wind, villagers plan for a stormy year; if she arrives on a sunny day, a drought is forecast; and her appearance on a rainy day indicates that times of plenty and rich harvests are forthcoming.[8]

Pay close attention whenever Yeongdeung Halmang blows seeds and shells into your life. Her arrival foretells the outcome of your endeavors. Now is the time to establish equilibrium between work, play, and ritual.

EAST

Set the table in preparation for a guest of honor, for she will bring abundant support to your ideas. The Korean wind ritual contains three parts: a welcome rite, a farewell rite, and preparation for Yeongdeung Halmang's visit to Soseom (Udo), or Cow Island, where Grandmother Yeongdeung is said to stay for one day before returning home.[9] In preparation for this ceremony, the sacred site is decorated with five long colored streamers and many food-laden tables featuring special oblong flat rice cakes, specially prepared for the grandmother. The shamans dance while symbolically opening a storage chest as an invitation for the ancestors (gods/goddesses) to enter and participate. Ritual bells, incense, a sacred fan, dance, and songs are used to entice and entertain Grandmother Yeongdeung. The time has arrived to prepare for a new cycle of personal growth.

Members of the community hoped that Yeongdeung Halmang would feed on the rice cakes, to satiate herself and bring temperate winds. It is time to ask, "What beliefs am I feeding, and what is the motivation for my goals?"

SOUTH

If Yeongdeung Halmang arrives from the south, invitations are forthcoming. In Jeju, the *olle* is the path between the house and the village. Grandmother has cleared the way for new beginnings, but are you emotionally prepared?

It is time to embark on a dive deep within, and to find your inner strength. Good fortune awaits you, but you may have to swim far beneath the surface of the ocean to acquire it. Yeongdeung Halmang brings good fortune when she blows in from the south, so be sure to express your gratitude for the typhoons, abundant shellfish, and crops she provides.

Greed is an undesirable and punishable trait in Korea. If you are planning a new enterprise or thinking of starting a new relationship, and the chilly winds of Yeongdeung Halmang suddenly appear, make sure your intentions are noble. Intense desire can be a sign of a blind spot, which may require the guidance of a wise counselor. If you believe your happiness is dependent on having more money, sex, fame, and possessions, then you need to reassess your outlook on life.

WEST

Balance requires give and take. Yeongdeung Halmang arrives as a consummate negotiator when she blows in from the west. She offers you physical rewards, but to receive them, you must release yourself from people, places, and things that no longer serve your best interests.

Materialism can be a source of unhappiness. Are you like a squirrel that's stockpiling nuts in anticipation of a long winter? If you had to evacuate your home in 30 minutes, what would you take with you? It's time to determine what is extraneous in your inner and outer worlds, and then clean house.

NORTH

When Yeongdeung Halmang rushes in from the north, you are being invited to dance with the ancestors. Community ritual is a powerful force that sustains life. In order to gain consensus in any situation, there must be a buy-in from the stakeholders. For more than 10,000 years, during times of peace and chaos, islanders were able to preserve their community rituals by listening to the wise counsel of their ancestors.

Grandmother is alerting you to broaden your awareness and be of service to something greater than yourself. Ask, "Am I being of service to others as well as to myself?" Open your eyes, mind, heart, and soul. Give of yourself unconditionally so that others may benefit from your kindness and generosity.

NO WIND (EQUATOR)

Doldrums

When you need a break,
invoke this pause: the energy of stillness, death.

Most cultures around the world have an expression for "no wind." According to Homer, no wind ever shook the peace at Mount Olympus; this heavenly spot was a sacred, peaceful refuge for the gods. In Polynesia, *haole* is a slang term used to describe foreigners who are lacking in breath, wind, or spirit.[1] To a Buddhist, the state of *nirvana*, which means "no wind," is a sacred place beyond ego consciousness. In the Bible, wind is synonymous with the Holy Spirit, which leaves the physical body upon death. Aristotle marked two specific points on the compass card, southeast and southwest, as "No Wind." These points signify places of stillness where there is no opposition from local crosswinds.

Attempting to tame disruptive winds is a common theme in native folktales worldwide. In one Hopi tale, the protagonist uses cornmeal to block the opening of a wind cave at Sunset Crater. In a Chippewa story, Nanabozho seeks revenge on his enemy by commanding the wind to be still and allow the heat of the sun to boil the waters of the lake. A Penobscot tale speaks of fierce winds interfering with Gluscabi's duck hunting. In response, the woodchuck binds the wings of the wind eagle to stop him from blowing. To avoid further destruction, Gluscabi liberates the bird with an agreement: "It is good that the wind should blow sometimes and other times it is good that it should be still."[2]

Although the importance of a flowing breeze cannot be denied, moments of calm and stillness can serve as opportunities for personal spiritual growth. These gaps in space and time are rest points in eternity—much like midnight, when one day ends and a new day begins. On windless seas, sailors drift. No Wind signifies stillness, silence, and suspended activity. In the same way, there are rest points between the inhalation and exhalation of breath, during which nature orchestrates tranquil spaces in your life. As Claude Debussy expressed, "Music is the space between the notes." In nature, timing is everything; that is why comedians pause before delivering the punchline.

No Wind is a blank space that exists between every cycle. Every project, relationship, and experience in life has a natural rhythm that includes birth, growth, death, and regeneration. One who has fully awakened cherishes each moment as a precious gift from spirit. You can resist this energy or choose to wait patiently until conditions change.

When the wind in your life comes to a standstill, be like a wise sailor, patiently waiting for the winds to shift.

EAST

If the wind leaves your sails and you find yourself stranded in the east, it is time to pause and reflect. As you drift, ask spirit to help you extinguish old, long-held ideas. Now is not the time to pray and request a new vision. Drifting presents an opportunity to enter higher realms of consciousness.

Spirit's blessing is essential for your plans to sprout and develop. Whether you are relocating to a new city, starting a new job, entering into a new relationship, or embarking on an adventure, you must align your beliefs to the will of spirit in order to succeed.

SOUTH

Efforts to trek across your emotional waters will lead to frustration. Now is not time to pick up the oars and paddle furiously. Relax, retreat, and surrender. Clean your house, go for a walk, write in your journal, cry up a river, watch a funny movie, or have a deep heartfelt conversation with someone you trust. Know that this too shall pass. Accepting and embracing emptiness will allow you to navigate safely through life's trials and tribulations.

Spirit may use No Wind to wake you up or jolt you out of a stupor. In Greek mythology, King Agamemnon's army put their ships out to sea once the wind died down. In the play *Iphigenia in Aulis* by Euripides, the goddess Artemis punishes Agamemnon for killing a deer in her sacred forest while boasting of his hunter prowess. He appeases her by sacrificing his daughter. Examine your actions to determine if you are bragging or resisting the divine guidance of spirit. You may be called upon to make a sacrifice. Are you willing to surrender and relinquish control for the good of the whole?

WEST

Rewards, gifts, and celebrations may be suspended when the wind decimates your western slope. This may manifest as the annihilation of illusions and long-held beliefs. A cycle is about to end. You may be experiencing a health issue, or a project may come to an abrupt end.

You have reached a physical plateau—but don't interpret this as the end of your journey, a lack of progress, or a setback. This is a time for calm and patience. Deep, subtle forces are healing and rejuvenating your body. Rest is an essential step in any cycle of change. Surrender to the calm, peaceful energy of No Wind, and allow it to restore your biological clock to its natural rhythm.

NORTH

No Wind represents seeds hibernating during winter, waiting for the perfect moment to sprout and enliven your life. No Wind is an invitation to open your heart and surrender to the divine. Remain humble. Trust in the invisible forces of nature.

When the winds cease to blow in the north, spiritual growth is forthcoming, as long as you are willing to trust and surrender.

In the Bible, God rested on the seventh day. Know that everything is perfectly aligned, balanced, and as it should be. Once a seed has been planted in fertile soil, a period of latency follows as the seed adjusts to its new environment. Know that when the time is right, the seeds you have planted will germinate, sprout, and thrive.

Some animals hibernate during winter to preserve their resources until spring arrives; this is an essential part of their life cycle. The stillness of No Wind shouldn't be viewed as stagnation or a waste of time, but as an opportunity to pause, reflect, and gain wisdom before moving on to the next chapter in your life. In the center of stillness resides a scintillating treasure trove of divine wisdom.

AFTERWORD

Deepening Wind Wisdom

I find myself transported back to a dark night when severe wind storms were brewing. The small cabin where I lived was meek in the face of the swaying branches of the 100-foot-tall pine sentinels that guarded our property. I prayed for harmony and for the safety of family, friends, and my home. My memory of that night showed me the truth of Catherine the Great's words about dodging falling branches and sweeping rains, and receiving a thorough wind lashing during a storm.

Wind is a sustaining life force on planet Earth. The arrival of the wind gods/goddesses described in this book, at this time in history, signals that we are ready to embark on a journey across the seas of change. We are standing on the threshold of the Anthropocene age, a time when our collective actions will either restore harmony on the planet or end life as we know it. I choose to believe in the innate goodness of human nature, that our collective "will" chooses harmony, and that we are beginning to "wake up." Still, the winds are blowing hard across our planet, and will continue to do so until we start listening.

We are all connected through breath, exhaled and carried around the world by the winds. Calling upon these winds helps us on our personal journeys through life. In my own experience, once I realized the winds had my back, I no longer felt the urge to control their movement. For the first time in my life I felt secure in the arms of spirit. I knew that if I continued to put into practice the skills I had acquired as I woke up, the winds would take care of the rest. Once I yielded to their wisdom and power, their mission became clear to me.

It is time to restore faith in the unseen. It has proven, time and time again, that living in harmony with nature ensures peace on earth. One of the key elements of nature is wind. Wind is the steady, powerful proof of the existence of spirit. Breathe in, breathe out, and feel your connection. Open the window, or even better, step out into nature. Just like the birds flying overhead, you are part of the great cycle of life on the planet. Let the wind energize, inspire, and guide you in the same manner that it motivates so many birds to fly southward for the winter.

It is my hope that you will find this book to be a constant companion and friend, and that you will see that the inner and outer winds are constantly moving through your life. Regularly employ the exercises outlined in this book and repeat them as needed. If you are feeling lost, visit one or more winds in Part IV and ask them for the support, guidance, and wisdom you need to navigate successfully through life, no matter which way the winds may be blowing.

ENDNOTES

Introduction

1. James Kale McNeley, *Holy Wind in Navajo Philosophy* (Tucson, AZ: University of Arizona Press, 1982),10.

2. Inga Kiderra, "Second Largest Maya Jade Found in Belize Has Unique Historical Inscription," Phys.org, last modified February 24, 2017, https://phys.org/news/2017-02-largest-maya-jade-belize-unique.html.

Chapter 1

1. Marion Woodman, "Listening to Our Deepest Wisdom, Part One: The Soul's Vulnerability from Sounds True: Insights at the Edge," Podbay, last modified 2012, http://podbay.fm/show/307934313/e/1354660562?autostart=1.

2. Swami Vivekananda, *Bhakti Yoga: The Yoga of Love and Devotion* (Leeds, England: Celephaïs Press, 2003), 73.

3. Online Etymology Dictionary, accessed May 29, 2017, http://www.etymonline.com.

4. Thich Nhat Hanh, *Stepping into Freedom: An Introduction to Buddhist Monastic Training* (Berkeley, CA: Parallax Press, 1997), 19.

5. Emory Sekaquaptewa and Dorothy Washburn, "As a Matter of Practice . . . Hopi Cosmology in Hopi Life: Some Considerations for Theory and Method in Southwestern Archaeology," *Time and Mind* 2, no. 2 (2009): xx, doi: 10.2752/175169709x423682.

Chapter 2

1. Tino Ramirez, Book Review of *The Wind Gourd of La'amaomao, Sunday Honolulu Advertiser and Star Bulletin*, January 20, 1991, http://www2.hawaii.edu/~dennisk/texts/ramirezwindgourd.html.

2. Diane Huling (personal communication, November 26, 2016).

3. Caline Malek, "Desert Survival: Secrets of Ancient Bedouin Navigation," *The National*, last modified July 26, 2011, http://www.thenational.ae/news/uae-news/desert-survival-secrets-of-ancient-bedouin-navigation.

4. Adrian V. Bell et al., "Driving Factors in the Colonization of Oceania: Developing Island-Level Statistical Models to Test Competing Hypotheses," *American Antiquity* 80, no. 2 (April 1, 2015): 397–407. doi:10.7183/0002-7316.80.2.397.

Chapter 3

1. Abraham Lincoln, "Collected Works of Abraham Lincoln. Volume 2," accessed July 19, 2016, http://quod.lib.umich.edu/l/lincoln/lincoln2/1:483.1?rgn=div2;view=fulltext.

2. The words first appeared in print in *Mother Goose's Melody* (London, c. 1765), possibly published by John Newbery (1713–1767). Carpenter, H., & Prichard, M. (1984). *The Oxford Companion to Children's Literature*: Oxford University Press.

3. Graham Hancock, *Magicians of the Gods: The Forgotten Wisdom of Earth's Lost Civilization* (New York: Thomas Dunne Books, 2015), 67.

4. Hancock, *Magicians of the Gods*, 47.

5. Xavier Rodóa et al., "Tropospheric winds from northeastern China carry the etiologic agent of Kawasaki disease from its source to Japan," in *Proceedings of the National Academy of Sciences* (San Diego, CA: University of California, 2014).

Chapter 4

1. James Russell Lowell, *The Writings of James Russell Lowell: Literary and Political Addresses* (Charleston, SC: Houghton Mifflin Harcourt, 1980), 17.

2. Ralph Keyes, *The Quote Verifier: Who Said What, Where, and When* (New York: St. Martin's Griffin, 2007), 160.

3. Polyxeni Potter, "From My Rotting Body, Flowers Shall Grow, and I Am in Them, and That Is Eternity," *Emerging Infectious Diseases* 17, no. 3 (March 2011): 573–574. doi:10.3201/eid1703.ac1703.

4. Center for Nonviolent Communication, 2005 Feelings Inventory, accessed on the web, https://www.cnvc.org/sites/default/files/feelings_inventory_0.pdf.

The Winds of Fate

1. Ella Wheeler Wilcox, *World Voices* (New York: Hearst's International Library Company, 1916), 51.

Introduction to the Cardinal Winds

1. John Wesley Powell, Jesse Walter Fewkes, Matthew Williams Stirling, William Henry Holmes, Frederick Webb Hodge, Annual Report, Volume 27, Parts 1905-1906 (U.S. Government Printing Office, 1911), 121.

Chapter 5

1.   P. L. Travers, *Mary Poppins* (Boston: Houghton Mifflin Harcourt, 1997), 10.
2.   P. L. Travers, *Mary Poppins*, 6.

Chapter 6

1.   Joshua J. Mark, "The Myth of Adapa (Article)," Ancient History Encyclopedia, last modified February 23, 2011, http://www.ancient.eu/article/216/.
2.   Joshua J. Mark, "The Myth of Adapa."
3.   Paul U. Unschuld, Hermann Tessenow, and Jinsheng Zheng, *Huang Di Nei Jing Su Wen: An Annotated Translation of Huang Di's Inner Classic—Basic Questions*, Volume I (Berkeley, California: University of California Press, 2011), 340.

Chapter 7

1.   Percy Bysshe Shelley, "Ode to the West Wind," Poets.org, accessed March 7, 2017, https://www.poets.org/poetsorg/poem/ode-west-wind.
2.   Percy Bysshe Shelley, "Ode to the West Wind."

Chapter 8

1.   OSNOVA, Bible: King James Version (Book Baby, 2012), Mark 8:36.

Chapter 9

1.   Ursula K. Le Guin, *A Wizard of Earthsea* (Boston: Houghton Mifflin Harcourt, 2012), 63.
2.   James George Frazer, "The Magical Control of the Wind," in *The Golden Bough* (New York: Macmillan, 1922), 80.
3.   James George Frazer, "The Magical Control of the Wind," 80.
4.   Historique, accessed March 7, 2017, http://www.sifflets-en-terre-cuite.org/HtmlE/Hist/paleo.html.
5.   L. E. McCullough, *The Complete Irish TinWhistle Tutor, New & Revised* (New York: Oak Publications 1987).
6.   9waysmysteryschool, "AZTEC Death whistle," 9waysmysteryschool, last modified 2002, http://9waysmysteryschool.tripod.com/sacredsoundtools/id31.html.
7.   Loretta A. Cormier, Sharyn R. Jones, and Michele Myatt Quinn, *The Domesticated Penis: How Womanhood Has Shaped Manhood* (Tuscaloosa, AL: University of Alabama Press, 2015), 97.
8.   Diane Barker, *Tibetan Prayer Flags: Send Your Blessings on the Breeze* (Sydney, Australia: Lothian Books, 2003), 12.
9.   Chogyam Trungpa, *Shambhala: The Sacred Path of the Warrior* (Boston, MA: Shambhala Publications, 2009), 124.

10. Timothy Clark, The Prayer Flag Tradition (Redway, CA: Radiant Heart Studio), http://www.prayerflags.com/download/article.pdf.

11. The Peace Flag Project, "History of Tibetan Prayer Flags," accessed July 27, 2016, http://www.thepeaceflagproject.org/historyoftibetanflags.htm.

Chapter 10

1. Mary Ellen Chase, *Words of Wisdom and Quotable Quotes by Dr. A.N.P. Ummerkutty Chennai* (Bangalore, India: Sura College of Competition, 2004), 91.

Chapter 12

1. Wilfred G. Lambert, *Babylonian Wisdom Literature* (Winona Lake, IN: Eisenbrauns, 1996), 164.

2. John Robinson, *Archaeologia Graeca, or the Antiquities of Greece: Being an Account of the Manners and Customs of the Greeks, and Relating to Their Government, Magistracy, Laws, Judical Proceedings, Religion, Games, Military and Naval Affairs, Dress, Exercises . . .* (London: Forgotten Books, 2015), 10.

Chapter 14

1. William Shakespeare, *The Tragedy of Macbeth* (Concord, MA: William K. Bradford Co., 1994), 48.

2. James George Frazer, "The Magical Control of the Wind," in *The Golden Bough*, by James George Frazer (New York: Macmillan, 1922), 80.

3. A. J. Perry, *The Old People* (Thames River Press, June 30, 2014), 43.

Chapter 15

1. "Sri Kaleshwar: The Sai Yuga," Kaleshwar.org, last modified 2005, https://www.kaleshwar.org/en/lineage_saiyuga.

Introduction to the 29 Wind Gods/Goddesses

1. Gloria Durka, "Inter-Religious Education and Conversion in a Divided World: Perspectives from the United States," *Religiski-filozofiski raksti* XVI, no. 1 (2013): 11–37.

Amaunet

1. Joyce Tyldesley, "The Role of Women in Ancient Egypt," accessed December 19, 2016, https://www.library.cornell.edu/colldev/mideast/womneg.htm.

2. Geraldine Pinch, *Egyptian Mythology: A Guide to the Gods, Goddesses, and Traditions of Ancient Egypt* (New York: Oxford University Press, 2004), 100.

3. Jan Assmann and Anthony Alcock, *Egyptian Solar Religion in the New Kingdom: Re, Amun and the Crisis of Polytheism*, 2nd ed. (London: Kegan Paul International, 1995), 186.

4. Assmann and Alcock, *Egyptian Solar Religion in the New Kingdom*, 186.

5. Assmann and Alcock, *Egyptian Solar Religion in the New Kingdom*, 186.

6. Jan Assmann and David Lorton, *The Search for God in Ancient Egypt* (Ithaca, NY: Cornell University Press, 2001), 2.

7. Alan Richardson and John B. Walker, *The Inner Guide to Egypt: A Mystical Journey through Time & Consciousness* (Woodbury, MN: Llewellyn Worldwide, 2010), 6.

8. Ahmid Shamahd, *The Reaffirmation of the Revelation* (Bloomington, IN: Xlibris Corporation, May 2, 2013), xxi.

Bieg-Olmai

1. Ian Hodder, ed., *Archaeology as Long-Term History (New Directions in Archaeology)* (Cambridge, U.K.: Cambridge University Press, 1987), 26.

2. C. Nooteboom, "Sketch of the Former Religious Concepts of the Asele Lapps (the Southern Lapps)," *Bijdragen tot de taal-, land- en volkenkunde/Journal of the Humanities and Social Sciences of Southeast Asia* 117, no. 1 (January 1961): 118–140. doi:10.1163/22134379-90002198.

Cardea

1. Horatius M. Piscinus, "Cardea: Blessing the Doorway," *Religio et Pietas Blog*, June 10, 2011, http://www.patheos.com/blogs/religioromana/2011/06/cardea-blessing-the-doorway.

2. Mary Rebecca Bell, *The Cults in Ovid, Fasti I* (University of Chicago, Department of Classical Languages and Literatures, 1921), 8.

Dogoda

1. Robert Graves, "Introduction," in *New Larousse Encyclopedia of Mythology*, by Felix Guirard et al. (London: Hamlyn, 1969), v.

2. M. Ivanov, "Mesolithic Shamans," *Elder Mountain Dreaming Blog*, September 2, 2016, https://eldermountain.wordpress.com/category/slavic-weather-shaman.

3. Denny Kutylowski, "Polish Paganism," Polish Toledo—Archive of Okana, 2005, accessed September 2, 2016, http://www.polishtoledo.com/pagan.

Esaugetúh Emissee

1. "Robbie Ethridge, *Creek Country: The Creek Indians and Their World* (Chapel Hill, NC: UNC Press Book, 2004), 110.

2. Bill Grantham, *Creation Myths and Legends of the Creek Indians* (Gainesville, FL: University Press of Florida, 2002), 22.

3. Frank Joseph, "Mythological Themes Connecting to the Bronze Age to Classical World Images," in *The Atlantis Encyclopedia*, by Frank Joseph and Brad Steiger (Normal, IL: New Page Books, 2005), 110.

4. Joseph, "Mythological Themes Connecting to the Bronze Age to Classical World Images," 110.

5. Daniel G. Brinton, *The Myths of the New World (A Treatise on the Symbolism and Mythology of the Red Race of America)* (Boston, MA: IndyPublish.com, 2007), 242–243.

Feng Po Po

1. Herbert James Allen, *Early Chinese History: Are the Chinese Classics Forged?* (Classic Reprint) (London: Forgotten Books, 2015), 8.

2. Anne M. Birrell, *Chinese Mythology: An Introduction* (Baltimore: The Johns Hopkins University Press, 1999), 20.

Fūjin

1. Kadoya Atsushi and Yumiyama Tatsuya "Izanami," *Encyclopedia of Shinto,* accessed March 6, 2016, http://eos.kokugakuin.ac.jp/modules/xwords/entry.php?entryID=83.

Holle

1. Catherine Heath, "From Fairytale to Goddess: Frau Holle and the Scholars That Try to Reveal Her Origins," Academia.edu, May 13, 2013, accessed August 14, 2016, http://www.academia.edu/3548067/From_Fairytale_To_Goddess_Frau_Holle_And_The_Scholars_That_Try_To_Reveal_Her_Origins.

2. Heath. "From Fairytale to Goddess."

3. Mu-chou Poo, *Rethinking Ghosts in World Religions* (Boston: Brill, 2006), 123.

4. Mu-chou Poo, *Rethinking Ghosts in World Religions*, 123.

Ilmarinen

1. Ersev Ersoy, "Social Reality and Mythic Worlds: Reflections on Folk Belief and the Supernatural in James Macpherson's Ossian and Elias Lönnrot's Kalevala" (Ph.D. thesis, the University of Edinburgh, 2012), 47. http://hdl.handle.net/1842/7842.

2. Mary Ellen Snodgrass, *Encyclopedia of the Literature of Empire* (New York: Infobase Publishing, 2010), 161.

3. John Martin Crawford, "The Kalevala, The Epic Poem of Finland, into English," Project Gutenberg, last modified 1888, http://www.gutenberg.org/cache/epub/5186/pg5186-images.html.

Kari

1. Philo Laos Mills, *Prehistoric Religion; A Study in Pre-Christian Antiquity* (Sydney, Australia: Wentworth Press, 2016), 69.

2. Mills, *Prehistoric Religion*, 69.

3.   A. S. Mackenzie, *The Evolution of Literature* (New York: Thomas Y. Crowell & Company, 2009), 84.

4.   Walter William Skeat, *Malay Magic: An Introduction to the Folklore and Popular Religion of the Malay Peninsular* (New York: The Macmillian Company, 1900), 22.

5.   György Busztin, *The Legacy of the Barang People: An Exploration into the Puzzling Similarities of the Hungarian and Malay Languages* (Jakarta: Equinox Publishing, 2006), 7.

La'amaomao

1.   "The Hawaiian Tradition of Pakaa and Ku-a-Pakaa, the Trusted Attendants of Keawenuiaumi, the King of Hawaii, and the Grandson of Laamaomao!," Hoakalei Cultural Foundation, 2014, accessed June 19, 2016, http://www. hoakaleifoundation.org/documents/hawaiian-tradition-pakaa-and-ku-pakaa-trusted-attendants-keawenuiaumi-king-hawaii-and.

2.   Katherine Roseguo and Anela Benson, *Mana Makani: The Power of the Wind* (Honolulu, HI: Bernice Pauahi Bishop Museum, 2014), http://resources. bishopmuseumeducation.org/resource_type/lesson/LM_Power_of_the_Wind_V04.pdf.

3.   Dennis Kawaharada, "Introduction to *The Wind Gourd of La'amaomao*," 1992, accessed on the web, http://www2.hawaii.edu/~dennisk/texts/introwindgourd.html.

4.   Niklaus R. Schweizer, review of *The Wind Gourd of La'amaomao*, by Moses Kuaea Nakuina, *The Hawaiian Journal of History* 25, no. 199: 212–215.

5.   Schweizer, review of *The Wind Gourd of La'amaomao*, 212–215.

Mari

1.   Ramón Zallo, *Basques, Today: Culture, History and Society in the Age of Diversity and Knowledge* (Irun, Spain: Alberdania, 2007), 131.

2.   Paul Hardwick and David Kennedy, *The Survival of Myth: Innovation, Singularity and Alterity* (Newcastle, U.K.: Cambridge Scholars Pub., 2014), 48.

3.   Hardwick and Kennedy, *The Survival of Myth: Innovation, Singularity and Alterity*, 47.

4.   Margaret Read MacDonald, ed., *Traditional Storytelling Today: An International Sourcebook* (London: Routledge, 2013), accessed June 2017, https://books. google.com/books?id=IFNcAgAAQBAJ.

Nilch'i

1.   Peter Iverson and Monty Roessel, *Diné: A History of the Navajos* (Albuquerque: University of New Mexico Press, 2002), 18.

2. Iverson and Roessel, *Diné*, 18.

3. James Kale McNeley, *Holy Wind in Navajo Philosophy* (Tucson, AZ: University of Arizona Press, 1982), 42.

4. McNeley, *Holy Wind in Navajo Philosophy*, 44.

Njörðr

1. William Alexander Craigie, *The Religion of Ancient Scandinavia* (London: Archibald Constable and Co., Ltd., 1906), 29.

Oyá

1. Baba Ifa Karade, *The Handbook of Yoruba Religious Concepts* (Iowa City, IA: Red Wheel/Weiser, 1994), xiii.

2. Karade, *The Handbook of Yoruba Religious Concepts*, xiii.

Shu

1. Geraldine Pinch, *Egyptian Mythology: A Guide to the Gods, Goddesses, and Traditions of Ancient Egypt* (New York: Oxford University Press, 2004), 14–15.

2. Pinch, *Egyptian Mythology*, 135.

3. Pinch, *Egyptian Mythology*, 65.

Sila Innua

1. Christine Selda, "Angakut-Expressive Arts Shamanism," Master's thesis. European graduate school EGS, 2014, accessed June 2017, http://mountainshamanism.com/thesis-angakut-expressive-arts-shamanism.

2. John Edward Huth, *The Lost Art of Finding Our Way* (Cambridge, MA: Harvard University Press, 2013), 13.

3. Huth, *The Lost Art of Finding Our Way*, 53.

4. Huth, *The Lost Art of Finding Our Way*, 14.

5. Huth, *The Lost Art of Finding Our Way*, 16.

Tāwhirimātea

1. K. R. Howe, "Story: Ideas of Māori origins," Te Ara—The Encyclopedia of New Zealand, accessed August 8, 2017, https://teara.govt.nz/en/ideas-of-maori-origins.

Tňaté

1. Nick White Swan, *Sun Dancer*, personal communication, September 26, 2016.

2. James R. Walker, *Lakota Myth* (Lincoln, NE: University of Nebraska Press, 1983), 369.

3.   D. M. Dooling and James R. Walker, *The Sons of the Wind: The Sacred Stories of the Lakota* (Norman, OK: University of Oklahoma Press, 1984).

Vayu

1.   Alain Daniélou, *The Myths and Gods of India: The Classic Work on Hindu Polytheism for the Inner Traditions*, 2nd ed. (Rochester, VT: Inner Traditions Bear and Company, 1991), 91.

2.   David Frawley, "Vayu Rahasya: The Secret of Vayu," American Institute of Vedic Studies, June 13, 2012, accessed May 15, 2015, http://vedanet.com/2012/06/13/vayu-rahasya-the-secret-of-vayu.

Vēja Māte

1.   Tupesu Janis, "The Ancient Latvian Religion—Dievturiba," ed. Vilius L. Dundzila, *Lithuanian Quarterly Journal of Arts and Sciences* 33, no. 3 (1987), June 2017, http://www.lituanus.org/1987/87_3_06.htm.

2.   Marija Alseikaite Gimbutas, *The Balts* (London: Thames and Hudson, 1963), 12.

3.   Ludis Adamovičs, *Ancient Latvian Reliģija*, 1937, zagarins.net.

4.   Janis, "The Ancient Latvian Religion—Dievturiba."

5.   Janis, "The Ancient Latvian Religion—Dievturiba."

6.   Gimbutas, *The Balts*, 96.

7.   Janis, "The Ancient Latvian Religion—Dievturiba."

8.   Gimbutas, *The Balts*, 96.

Wayramama

1.   Daniel Brinton, *The Myths of the New World* (Philadelphia: The Library of Alexandria, 1868), 52.

2.   Patt O'Neill, "Glossary of Terminology of the Shamanic & Ceremonial Traditions of the Inca Medicine Lineage," Incaglossary.org, 2014, accessed July 15, 2015, http://www.incaglossary.org/a.html.

3.   Elizabeth Jenkins, author, personal communication, September 26, 2015.

Yaponcha

1.   Edmund Nequatewa, *Truth of a Hopi* (New York: Start Publishing, 2012), foreword.

2.   Harold Courlander, *The Fourth World of the Hopis: The Epic Story of the Hopi Indians as Preserved in Their Legends and Traditions*, 9th ed. (Albuquerque: University of New Mexico Press, 1987), 10.

3.   Emory Sekaquaptewa and Dorothy Washburn. "As a Matter of Practice . . . Hopi Cosmology in Hopi Life: Some Considerations for Theory and Method in Southwestern Archaeology," *Time and Mind: The Journal of Archaeology, Consciousness and Culture* 2, no. 2, July 2009, 4.

Yel Ana

1. Lucy J. Reid, *She Changes Everything: Seeking the Devine on a Feminist Path* (London: Continuum International Publishing Group, 2006), 6.

Yeongdeung Halmang

1. Dr. Anne Hilty, personal communication, December 22, 2016.

2. Dr. Anne Hilty, "Yeongdeung Halmang, Goddess of wind and sea." *The Jeju Weekly*, March 25, 2013, http://www.jejuweekly.com/news/articleView. html?idxno=3036.

3. "The Legend of Jeju´s Origin," Jeju Tourism Organization, accessed July 11, 2016, http://www.ijto.or.kr/english/index.php?cid=17.

4. Andrea DenHoed, "The Sea Women of South Korea," *The New Yorker*, March 29, 2015, http://www.newyorker.com/culture/photo-booth/ sea-women-of-south-korea.

5. DenHoed, "The Sea Women of South Korea."

6. National Folk Museum of Korea, "Wind God Festival," Encyclopedia of Korean Folk Culture, accessed July 11, 2016, http://folkency.nfm.go.kr/eng/ twelvemonths.jsp?id=695&d=&m=february.

7. Anne Hilty, personal communication, December 22, 2016.

8. National Folk Museum of Korea, "Wind God Festival," http://folkency.nfm. go.kr/eng/twelvemonths.jsp?id=695&d=&m=february.

9. Dr. Anne Hilty, "Yeongdeung Halmang, Goddess of wind and sea." *The Jeju Weekly*, March 25, 2013, http://www.jejuweekly.com/news/articleView. html?idxno=3036.

No Wind

1. Charles W. Kenn, "What is a Haole?" *Paradise of the Pacific*, August 1944, 16.

2. Gluscabi and the Wind Eagle, an Abenaki Legend, accessed on the web. http://www.firstpeople.us/FP-Html-Legends/GluscabiandtheWindEagle-Abenaki.html.

ACKNOWLEDGMENTS

Wind creates movement in our imagination, emotions, body, and spirit. While one sail can catch an inspiring wind, moving a ship requires a crew. At the first faint stirring of the wind, two visionaries encouraged wind work. Early on, book magi Stephanie Gunning helped me to develop the concept during several incarnations of the book proposal. Process doula Suzanne Fageol helped me organize these ancient practices so they would become relevant systems for navigating change and healing in the modern world. Later, as the crazy creative winds told me their stories, poet Jean-Pierre Raven Gregoire became my writing companion. He finessed my chaotic words, asking me to clarify the text point by point during our many Skype sessions. Two years into the process, he proclaimed, "You have created a whole new system of healing." Because he understood what I was trying to accomplish with my wind work, I now trust that others will understand it too. It takes a wise village to birth the wind; additional editing insight was provided by Vrinda Pendred and longtime friend Debra Kamino.

I am grateful to the staff at Hay House. Wise woman Patricia Gift, a longtime friend and vice president, editorial, of Hay House, would add encouraging input annually. One sentence would reshape the entire project. After four years, her winds stirred; she looked up from lunch and said, "You are writing a book that has not been written." I am grateful for the trout we shared after our rigorous mountain journey in Peru, and all our meals since. Thank you, Sally Mason-Swaab, for your warm embrace of these winds of spirit; your guidance through the book birthing made this process a breeze.

One day during a lecture, Swami Kaleshwar told us, "A soul mate is someone who has your back, no matter what." I am eternally grateful for mine, longtime friend Lisa Weit, who has supported every crazy twist and turn in my life for over twenty years, and who provided the Owls Den island retreat.

This book has also been made possible because teachers appeared along the way to help me heal and change my perception. These include: Lakota teachers Becky and Richard Sais, Maria Teresa Valenzuela, Alberto Villoldo, Sandra Ingerman, Linda Fitch, Jose Luis Herrera, Cindy Lyndsay-Rael, Luzia, Elizabeth Jenkins, Hank Wesselman, and Brooke Medicine Eagle, whose book I stumbled upon first. I am eternally grateful to my brother-in-law Joe, whose confirmation that I was part of the family, no matter what, and to get over myself, began healing the rifts I had always felt.

Thank you to my mom, who modeled the values of hard work and perseverance.

When you are very clear on your vision, the winds conspire to help. Thank you to Krista Gilbert, Ph.D., group CEO at Foundations Recovery Network, and Craig McLaughlin, LMFT, for allowing the winds to dance through my work/writing experience. Sophie Stenbeck, your generous love and support throughout the process and your presence makes the world a better place for all. Thank you, Elizabeth Danes and Bea Bensinger, for believing in this book and me; your spirits took flight during the process, but you live on in the wind. Barbara Lucas, your insightful read, wisdom, and ability to feel and see these gods/goddesses opened my vision to the unseen world of wind.

It takes a village. Mine includes: Teresa Newell, Cindy Muller, Anka Jovanovic, Lori Lothian, Debra Savitt, Gala Mitchell, Arlette Capel, Lisa Weikel, Susan Reiner, Pamela Kenney, Audrey Reed, Rev Sharon Stroud, Brenda Burger, Mario Donato, and Elana Shay; each of you has played a pivotal role in shaping the life of this book. Thank you to Christopher Knippers, Ph.D., for your kind and perceptive read.

Finally, sincere gratitude to the members of the Facebook Wind Believers group, who have invited the wind gods/goddesses into their lives and faithfully tested these processes.

ABOUT THE AUTHOR

Renee Baribeau is a wind whistler, soul coach, author, inspirational speaker, entrepreneur, and workshop leader, known and respected for her down-to-earth approach. During her life, the wind gods have steered Renee's course in many directions. A former chef, in 1987 she opened the first farm-to-table restaurant in Central New York, Brown Bagger's in Syracuse. In 2005, Renee established the Desert Holistic Network in Palm Desert, California, an online regional resource directory. Renee served as the resident shaman at We Care Spa in Desert Hot Springs. Since 2013, Renee has worked for Foundations Recovery Network, a national system of residential treatment facilities. Her current role is marketing and community outreach coordinator.

As a writer, Renee is a featured contributing blogger for FinerMinds and *Elephant Journal*. Renee has also contributed chapters to the anthologies *Pearls of Wisdom: 30 Inspirational Ideas to Live Your Best Life Now* (Hierophant Publishing, 2012) and *The Five Principles of Everything* (Five Birds Publishing, 2012). She makes her home on the West Coast and Whidbey Island.

We hope you enjoyed this Hay House book. If you'd like to receive our online catalog featuring additional information on Hay House books and products, or if you'd like to find out more about the Hay Foundation, please contact:

Hay House, Inc., P.O. Box 5100, Carlsbad, CA 92018-5100
(760) 431-7695 or (800) 654-5126
(760) 431-6948 (fax) or (800) 650-5115 (fax)
www.hayhouse.com® • www.hayfoundation.org

———

Published in Australia by: Hay House Australia Pty. Ltd.,
18/36 Ralph St., Alexandria NSW 2015
Phone: 612-9669-4299 • *Fax:* 612-9669-4144
www.hayhouse.com.au

Published in the United Kingdom by: Hay House UK, Ltd.,
The Sixth Floor, Watson House, 54 Baker Street, London W1U 7BU
Phone: +44 (0)20 3927 7290 • *Fax:* +44 (0)20 3927 7291
www.hayhouse.co.uk

Published in India by: Hay House Publishers India,
Muskaan Complex, Plot No. 3, B-2, Vasant Kunj, New Delhi 110 070
Phone: 91-11-4176-1620 • *Fax:* 91-11-4176-1630
www.hayhouse.co.in

———

Access New Knowledge.
Anytime. Anywhere.

Learn and evolve at your own pace
with the world's leading experts.

www.hayhouseU.com

Printed in the United States
by Baker & Taylor Publisher Services